GCSE 9–1

SPELLING, PUNCTUATION & GRAMMAR REVISION GUIDE

Annabel Wall

Subject-specific content:
Rose Taylor (Geography)
Annabel Wall (English literature)
Charlotte Gallimore (History)
Wendy Prosser (Religious studies)

Author Annabel Wall
Subject-specific content authors
Annabel Wall (English literature), Rose Taylor (Geography),
Charlotte Gallimore (History), Wendy Prosser (Religious studies)

Editorial team Susannah Fountain, Rachel Morgan, Vicki Yates
Series designers emc design ltd
Typesetting Couper Street Type Co.
App development Hannah Barnett, Phil Crothers, Haremi Ltd and Raiosoft International Private Limited.

Designed using Adobe InDesign
Published by Scholastic Education, an imprint of Scholastic Ltd, Book End, Range Road, Witney, Oxfordshire, OX29 0YD
Registered office: Westfield Road, Southam, Warwickshire CV47 0RA
www.scholastic.co.uk

Printed by Bell & Bain Ltd, Glasgow
© 2019 Scholastic Ltd
1 2 3 4 5 6 7 8 9   9 0 1 2 3 4 5 6 7 8

British Library Cataloguing-in-Publication Data
A catalogue record for this book is available from the British Library.
ISBN 978-1407-18269-8

Acknowledgements
The publishers gratefully acknowledge permission to reproduce the following copyright material:
Photos: p9: Thinkglass/Shutterstock; p13: TungCheung/Shutterstock; p17: Claudio Divizia/Shutterstock; p29: advent/Shutterstock; p30: RuslanaTimchenko/Shutterstock; p37: Nelson/Shutterstock; p41: Noi1990/Shutterstock; p54: StunningArt/Shutterstock; p67: arrowsmith2/Shutterstock
Cartoons: p32: Ron McGeary/Cartoonstock; p38: Jim Naylor/Cartoonstock; p49: Chris Wildt/Cartoonstock

Contents

How to use this book

Inside this Revision Guide you will find everything you need to help you revise the Spelling, Punctuation and Grammar (SPaG) rules and techniques to use in your 9-1 GCSEs.

The best way to retain information is to take an active approach to revision. Throughout this book, you will find lots of features that will make your revision an active, successful process.

SNAP IT!

Use the revision app to take pictures of key concepts and information. Great for revision on the go!

DO IT!

Activities to embed your knowledge and understanding and prepare you for the exams.

SUPPORT IT!

Reminders and tips to help you revise tricky SPaG points.

NAIL IT!

Tips written by subject experts to help you in the revision process.

STRETCH IT!

Content that stretches you further.

Callouts Additional explanations of important points.

CONTEXTUALISE IT!

Content which puts rules and examples into a subject-specific context.

Use the Spelling, Punctuation and Grammar Practice Book alongside the Revision Guide to get you exam ready!

CHECK IT!

Check your knowledge by answering questions at the end of each section.

FREE REVISION APP

- The **free revision app** can be downloaded to your mobile phone (iOS and Android), making **on-the-go revision** easy.

- Use the revision calendar to help map out your revision in the lead-up to the exam.

- Complete multiple-choice questions and create your own **SNAP IT!** revision cards.

www.scholastic.co.uk/gcse

Introduction

The effective use of spelling, punctuation and grammar (SPaG) in your written work is important in all of your GCSE 9–1 exams. However, it is especially important in your English literature, geography, history and religious studies exams, as SPaG constitutes **five per cent** of the marks in these subjects.

Marks for SPaG will be allocated to certain questions and it will be clear on your exam paper which questions these are. Losing marks for poor spelling, punctuation and grammar could mean the difference of a grade to you.

The Revision Guide is not exam-board specific. It is intended to give you, not only the confidence to implement the correct SPaG techniques and rules when you write, but also to give you guidance on how to improve your writing.

Curriculum mapping

Your teachers will tell you the exam board that you are following, the specific exam you are studying for and the topics you are covering. You can look up each specification on the exam boards' websites. It is worth familiarising yourself with these so that you can see exactly where marks are allocated for accuracy in spelling, punctuation and grammar.

The assessment of SPaG covers two areas. Examiners are looking for students who can:

* spell, punctuate and use grammar accurately

* use subject-specific vocabulary and specialist terms accurately.

With this in mind, you will be assessed using the following performance level descriptions. You should therefore be aware of each level and how you can improve your work in order to gain the maximum marks available for SPaG.

High performance	Candidates spell, punctuate and use the rules of grammar with consistent accuracy and effective control of meaning in the context of the demands of the question. Where required, they use a wide range of specialist terms adeptly and with precision.
Intermediate performance	Candidates spell, punctuate and use the rules of grammar with considerable accuracy and general control of meaning in the context of the demands of the question. Where required, they use a good range of specialist terms with facility.
Threshold performance	Candidates spell, punctuate and use the rules of grammar with reasonable accuracy in the context of the demands of the question. Any errors do not hinder meaning in the response. Where required, they use a limited range of specialist terms appropriately.
No marks awarded	Errors severely hinder the meaning of the response or candidates do not spell, punctuate or use the rules of grammar within the context of the demands of the question.

Throughout the Revision Guide, references are made to the level descriptions.

HOW TO REVISE!

PLAN YOUR REVISION

Get ahead by planning your revision!

Work out the **time** you have available for revising.

Think about when you work at your best. Are you a morning or an evening person?

Allocate **MORE TIME** for the topics you struggle with.

Revision works best in **SMALL BURSTS**, so keep sessions **SHORT AND SWEET**!

Remember to allow time to **PRACTISE** applying what you have revised.

Use your **revision app** to put together a revision timetable.

LOOK AFTER YOURSELF

Help your brain by looking after your whole body!

Take regular **breaks** from revising – your brain needs time to digest information in order to retain it.

★ HOTEL ★

Keep **hydrated** by drinking plenty of water – dehydration stops your brain from working at its full capacity.

Regular **exercise** helps stimulate the brain and will help you relax.

Get plenty of **sleep**, especially the night before an exam.

EAT WELL and limit unhealthy snacks – your brain needs fuel for memory and concentration.

Find methods of **relaxation** that work for you throughout the revision period.

BE PREPARED!

Limit potential stress on the day of an exam by getting everything you need ready the night before.

30

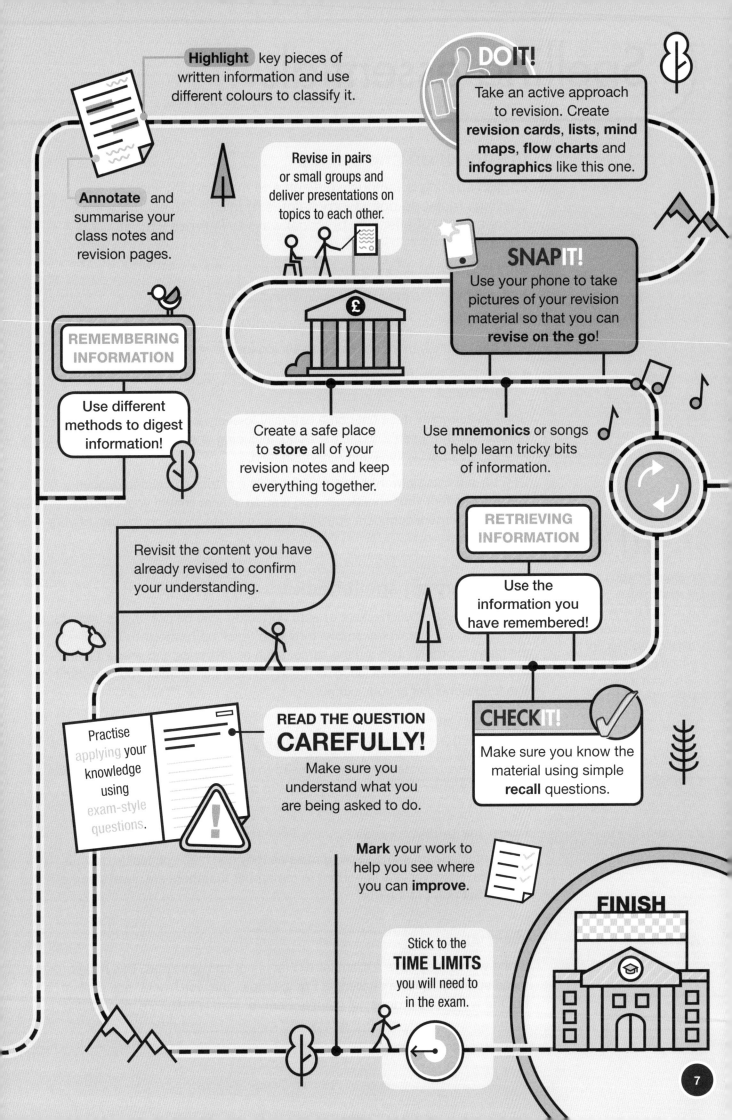

Highlight key pieces of written information and use different colours to classify it.

DO IT!
Take an active approach to revision. Create **revision cards**, **lists**, **mind maps**, **flow charts** and **infographics** like this one.

Annotate and summarise your class notes and revision pages.

Revise in pairs or small groups and deliver presentations on topics to each other.

SNAP IT!
Use your phone to take pictures of your revision material so that you can **revise on the go!**

REMEMBERING INFORMATION

Use different methods to digest information!

Create a safe place to **store** all of your revision notes and keep everything together.

Use **mnemonics** or songs to help learn tricky bits of information.

RETRIEVING INFORMATION

Use the information you have remembered!

Revisit the content you have already revised to confirm your understanding.

Practise applying your knowledge using exam-style questions.

READ THE QUESTION CAREFULLY!
Make sure you understand what you are being asked to do.

CHECK IT!
Make sure you know the material using simple **recall** questions.

Mark your work to help you see where you can **improve**.

FINISH

Stick to the **TIME LIMITS** you will need to in the exam.

Spelling essentials

Introduction and advice

English spelling is famously difficult and many adults find some spellings tricky, so don't worry if you struggle to use accurate spelling. There are lots of effective, practical ways to improve your spelling confidence.

Why is accurate spelling important?

- It can make the meaning of your writing clear.
- It can give you more confidence as a writer.
- It can create a more positive impression for the reader.
- If you use accurate spelling, you will also pick up more marks in some of your exams.

Spelling accuracy does not come naturally to everyone. Many famous thinkers and writers struggled with their spelling, including Winston Churchill, Jane Austen, Charles Dickens and Albert Einstein.

Don't avoid using a word because the spelling is tricky. Avoiding difficult words will affect your confidence and lead to a more limited vocabulary. Becoming a more confident speller will allow you to focus on the rest of your writing.

Don't rely on spellcheckers

Although digital spellcheckers or auto correctors can be useful, it is important not to rely on them. For example, they won't pick up **homophone** spelling mistakes (words that sound the same, such as *presence* and *presents*) and the misspelling of names (such as those of historical figures). You also can't use a spellchecker in your exam!

Strategies for learning tricky spellings

To become a confident speller, you need to use a combination of strategies and learn some rules in order to be able to spell and remember words.

Learn the rules

It is useful to learn some spelling rules as they can help you tackle difficult spellings. However, it is important to remember that there are always some words that don't fit the rule.

Silent letters

Some words may have a silent letter that is not spoken aloud. This makes these spellings quite a challenge. For example, the word 'debt' has a silent 'b' but the word 'debit' does not have a silent 'b' (and is therefore much easier to spell).

DO IT!

Every time you use a spellchecker, keep a note of the words that are underlined or highlighted. Record which part of the word is difficult for you.

- The most common silent letter is 'k' at the start of a word; the letter 'k' is always silent before an 'n'. These words **sound** like they start with an 'n' but actually start with the letters 'kn'. (For example: knight, know, knew, knowledge, knife, kneel, knot.)

- The other most common silent letter is 'w' at the start of a word (write, whole, wrong, wreck, wrinkle).

Silent letters can also appear in the middle or at the end of words. There are some patterns for these letters, so remembering them can make them easier to spot.

- The silent letter 'b' is often at the end of a word (for example, comb, lamb, numb, tomb, womb).

- The silent letter 'b' also often appears before a 't' (for example, subtle, debt and doubt).

- The silent letter 'd' is usually in the middle of a word (for example, Wednesday and handkerchief).

- The silent letter 'c' usually follows the letter 's' (for example, scene, scissors, scent, conscience, descend, fascinate).

- The silent letter 'e' is often found at the end of a word (for example, Bible and challenge).

- There is often a silent letter 'e' in the 'ed' ending of a word (for example, stopped, hopped).

Some words with silent letters don't follow a pattern, but it is useful to be aware of them when you're learning difficult spellings (for example, the word 'tsunami').

NAIL IT!

If you remember the silent letters 'k' and 'w' in your exam you will avoid many common spelling mistakes.

DO IT!

Rewrite the following sentences, correcting the silent letter spelling mistakes.

1 Do you now how to revise?
2 There is a very steep clime to the top of the mountain.
3 It's important to collect all your notes together befor you start to revise.
4 Did you hear that nock at the door?
5 The playright wants the audience to feel tense in this sene.
6 In the Bibl the students of Jesus are called disiples.

Allways chek for speling erors

Plural rules

It is very common to make spelling mistakes when using **plurals** (words that show more than one). There are quite a few rules to learn for plurals, but they can be a useful way to understand these tricky spellings.

The easiest plural is when you just add an 's' to the end of the word.

For example, the word *religion* becomes *religions* and the word *character* becomes *characters* and *mountain* becomes *mountains*.

For the following plural rules, it helps to know the difference between a **vowel** (a, e, i, o, u) and a **consonant** (all the other letters in the alphabet).

SNAPIT!

Plural word ends in….	What to look for...	What needs to be added or replaced...	Examples
y	Is there a vowel before the 'y'?	Just add 's'	valley = valleys essay = essays guy = guys There are some words that break this rule, for example, the word *soliloquy* becomes *soliloquies*.
	Is there a consonant before the 'y'?	Replace the 'y' with an 'ies'	city = cities history = histories spy = spies
o	Is there a vowel before the 'o'?	Just add 's'	radio = radios cameo = cameos video = videos stereo = stereos
	Is there a consonant before the 'o'?	Just add 'es'	volcano = volcanoes hero = heroes
sh ch x	These sounds are sometimes called 'hissing' or 'shushing' sounds.	Just add 'es'	church = churches wish = wishes mix = mixes
z		Just add 'zes'	quiz = quizzes buzz = buzzes
s	A word may already end with an 's'	Just add 'es'	loss = losses circus = circuses
fe f		Replace the 'f' or 'fe' with 'ves'	life = lives half = halves leaf = leaves wife = wives There are some awkward words that don't follow this rule, for example: belief = beliefs reef = reefs chef = chefs

Irregular plurals

Some words don't follow any of these rules, these are called irregular plurals.

Some plural words stay the same:

sheep – sheep	deer – deer	species – species
series – series	aircraft – aircraft	fish – fish

Some plurals change the word completely:

woman – women

person – people

mouse – mice

brother – brethren (although this old-fashioned plural is only used in a religious context)

foot – feet

tooth – teeth

Some plural words have no singular:

trousers   scissors   tropics

i before e (except after c)

This is a well-known spelling rule that can sometimes be useful. For example, a word like *believe* is often spelled incorrectly and this rule could help you remember the tricky part of the spelling. However, as with most spelling rules, it is important to remember that there are some words that don't follow the rule.

Words that follow the rule:

siege	belief	piece
shield	conceit	perceive
friend	believe	thief
hierarchy	deceit	receipt
achieve	chief	yield
ceiling	deceive	receive

Some words that don't follow the rule:

reign	glacier
seismic	weight
ancient	neighbour
foreign	

 **STRETCH**IT!

Playing Scrabble (either online or as a board game) is an excellent way to challenge your spelling accuracy. Choose an opponent who has a wide vocabulary.

Suffix rules

A suffix is a group of letters added to the end of a word to change the meaning. It is common to misspell the suffix of a word, but there are some useful patterns and rules to help you.

Dropping the e before adding a suffix: The 'e' is usually dropped from a word before adding a suffix that starts with a vowel, like *ing*.

SNAP IT!

Suffix	Word		Drop the 'e' before adding the suffix		Exceptions – words that don't fit this pattern	
'ing'	close	stare	closing	staring	fleeing	being
	hope	write	hoping	writing	canoeing	agreeing
	come		coming		seeing	
'ed'	hope	smile	hoped	smiled		
	change	raise	changed	raised		
'able'	excite	adore	excitable	adorable		
	believe		believable			

Keeping the 'e' before adding a suffix: However, some words with a vowel suffix *keep* the 'e'. For example, words ending in 'ce' or 'qe'

knowledge = knowledgeable   notice = noticeable

courage = courageous   manage = manageable

If you are adding a consonant suffix you also usually *keep* the 'e'. These words are often misspelled.

SNAP IT!

Suffix	Word		Keep the 'e' when adding a suffix		Exceptions – words that don't fit this pattern
'ly'	love	separate	lovely	separately	truly
	lone	definite	lonely	definitely	
'less'	care	taste	careless	tasteless	
	name	use	nameless	useless	
'ment'	excite	manage	excitement	management	argument
	judge	encourage	judgement	encouragement	
			The word *argument* does not follow this rule, as it does drop the 'e'.		

Other suffix endings

It is common to confuse the word endings 'tion', 'cian' and 'sion' because they all have a similar sound. Try to remember patterns for these groups of words to help you remember which one to use. For example, words about occupations often have a 'ian' suffix.

musician

comedian

politician

historian

optician

mathematician

There are other word endings that cause confusion for spellers. For example, you might mix up 'ent' with 'ant' and 'ence' with 'ance'. It often helps to create pairs of words for these endings:

ent/ence endings

intellig**ent** – intellig**ence**

innoc**ent** – innoc**ence**

magnifi**cent** – magnifi**cence**

ant/ance endings

hesit**ant** – hesit**ance**

toler**ant** – toler**ance**

domin**ant** – domin**ance**

STRETCH IT!

What other pairs can you find with these word endings? Create your own lists and learn the endings that you find difficult to remember.

CONTEXTUALISE IT!

This geography student spells with *reasonable accuracy in the context of the demands of the question* and therefore would be assessed on spelling at the Threshold performance. This student has made suffix mistakes which mean that the spelling cannot be judged to have *considerable accuracy* (Intermediate performance).

> Mount Etna is an active volcano and frequently disrupts the lifes of those living nearby. The citys of Catania and Caltanissetta are often disrupted by volcanic activity. Agricultural work in the region's many vallys often has to cease which impacts on local businesses. However, the volcano's activity can boost the economys of tourism enterprises which are increasingly being relied upon on the island of Sicily.

suffix /ˈsʌfɪks/ nou
letters that you add
make another wor

Remembering double letters

Forgetting to double a letter is usually because you can't always **hear** it.

There is no set of rules for many double-letter words, so the most useful approach is to learn some common examples:

balloon | embarrass | possession

disappoint | essential | success

different | tomorrow | committee

occurred | immediate

The C-V-C Rule (Consonant-Vowel-Consonant)

Forgetting to double a letter is a common mistake when adding a suffix (for example, sto**pp**ed).

The C-V-C rule could help you remember when to double a letter. If the last three letters of a word are a consonant, followed by a vowel, followed by a consonant (like for<u>get</u> or s<u>hop</u>), then the last letter is normally doubled before adding a suffix (forget = forge**tt**ing, shop = sho**pp**ing).

There are some awkward words that **don't** fit this rule. If the first syllable of a word is stressed, like <u>open</u>ing, then you **don't** double the letter when adding a suffix (even if it follows the C-V-C rule).

The letters c, h, q, w, x, y are never or rarely doubled when adding a suffix.

Mistakenly doubling letters

A common mistake is to double a consonant when it is **not** needed. For example, adding an extra 'l' to 'always' to make the incorrect spelling of 'allways'. This mistake is often made because it **sounds** like the word starts with 'all'. Another common mistake is to double the letter 'm' in tomorrow.

You will just have to learn your own list of tricky spellings. There is advice about how to remember individual spellings later in this chapter.

Very few suffix words end with a double 'll'. The word 'full' always drops the second 'l' when it becomes a suffix (as in painful, hopeful, successful, faithful, merciful). This is a useful rule to learn so you avoid the mistake of adding a double 'l' at the end of a word.

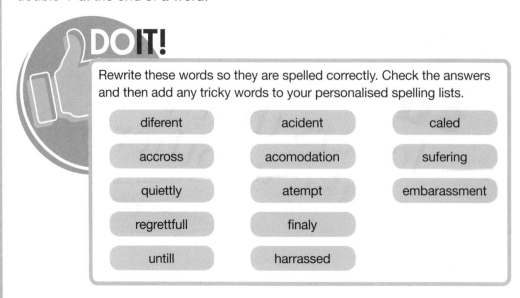

DOIT!

Rewrite these words so they are spelled correctly. Check the answers and then add any tricky words to your personalised spelling lists.

diferent | acident | caled

accross | acomodation | sufering

quiettly | atempt | embarassment

regrettfull | finaly

untill | harrassed

Learn the word

 SUPPORTIT!

Sometimes you simply need to learn a spelling off by heart. There are various ways to memorise a difficult spelling:

Use a memorable phrase or sentence

- rhythm – rhythm helps your two hips move.

- graph – get right and play hard

- necessary – there is one collar and two sleeves (to remember there is one 'c' and two 's')

- tomorrow – shall I go with Tom or row?

Find words within words

- There is a bra in the library!

- The words our and favour are in favourite.

- The word reign in foreign, sovereign.

- Never believe a lie.

Break up a word into sections or syllables

This can be a very effective way to cope with longer words. For example, international could become *in-ter-nation-al* (sections) and extravagant can become *ex-tra-va-gant* (syllables).

Look/say/remember/cover/write/check

This is a very common method for learning spellings. Although it is very simple, it can be very effective. This strategy is useful for learning a group of spellings that you frequently misspell.

This method works well because you can quickly test yourself on key spellings.

Make it bigger

It is very important to keep *looking* at the spelling you want to learn. If you are asked why you think a spelling is correct, you may say that '…it just looks right'. There is some evidence to suggest that making the word bigger helps your brain to remember the spelling and how it is meant to 'look'.

THINK BIG!

DOIT!

Make flash cards of the spellings that you find difficult and use a font that is several times bigger than your average type. This will allow you to focus on one word at a time and the increased size should aid your long-term memory.

Avoid focusing on misspelled words

When you create your personalised spelling lists, make sure all the words are spelled correctly. (Ask someone to check your list or use a dictionary to do it yourself.) Although it is helpful to identify which parts of the word are tricky, avoid focusing on lists of misspelled words.

STRETCH IT!

It is very useful to learn where words come from. If you learn how a word is built from an original meaning, it could help you spell and use more specialist vocabulary. For example, the word 'autobiography' is built from the following words:

- *auto* meaning self

- *bio* meaning life

- *graphy* meaning writing about.

Taking a general interest in the origins of words will widen your vocabulary and could help your spelling accuracy.

DO IT!

Your spelling confidence will improve if you focus on patterns in your own spelling mistakes. Try creating your own personalised list of spellings by following these steps:

1 Collect together examples of your own written work, such as exercise books, exam answers, homework, revision notes). Pick work from a range of your subjects (for example, history, English, religious studies and geography).
2 Look for any misspellings that have been highlighted by your teacher. If there are no spellings highlighted, ask a confident speller to check over your work and identify if there are any mistakes.
3 Using a dictionary, cross out the misspelling and add the correct word in a different colour. Make sure this word is written clearly in the margin.
4 Use this information to create your own personalised spelling lists – can you spot any patterns in your mistakes? Can any of the words be grouped together? (For example, you could group together words with a 'sion' or a 'tion' suffix.)
5 Re-read the spelling section of this guide. What rules might help you remember these spellings? (For example, the rules for plurals.)
6 What strategies can you use to learn the words from your spelling list? Pick three strategies from this section and experiment with them.
7 Focus on ten words at a time and test yourself regularly. When you've spelled a word correctly at least four times, replace it with another word
8 Monitor words that you are still finding tricky and experiment with strategies for learning them.

Writing errors

Make sure you use a clear space between words. Sometimes a word could appear to be a misspelling because it runs into the word before or after. It is also important to make sure your individual letters are clear when you write: you don't want to lose marks because the spelling of a word **looks** inaccurate.

NAILIT!

Don't use informal, shortened versions of words.

Many of the informal, shortened words used on social media are not appropriate in an exam. Although evidence shows that many students know when to avoid these words, sometimes they can creep into an exam answer.

For example:
- you = u
- thank you = thanx
- tomorrow = 2moro
- night = nite
- because = cos

Avoid any abbreviations unless they are specialist terms used in your GCSE subject. For example, in your geography exam it is acceptable to use EDC for Emerging Developing Country.

American and British spellings

In the early 20th century the USA officially changed some of its spellings to simplify words and make them easier to spell. It is important to be aware of the differences between American English and British English spellings. For example, many American words use a 'z' instead of an 's'.

SNAPIT!

British spelling	American spelling
centre	center
jewellery	jewelry
colour	color
analyse	analyze
neighbour	neighbor
labour	labor
theatre	theater

Remember to make sure that your spellchecker is set to British spelling or you may get into the habit of using American spelling.

DOIT!

Look carefully at the differences between British and American spelling. Can you spot any patterns?

Homophones

The most commonly misspelled words are homophones: words with the same sound, but different meaning and spelling.

There/their/they're

- The word *there* is a word about place. For example, *We are going over there to revise.*

- *They're* is a shortened version (a contraction) of *they are*. For example, *They're hoping to revise together in the afternoon.*

- *Their* is a possessive word. For example, *Their revision was going well.*

Your/you're

- *You're* is a shorted version of *you are*. For example, *You're focusing well on your revision tasks.*

- *Your* is a possessive word. For example, *Remember to bring your revision timetable.*

Here/hear

- Remember this word within a word: the word *hear* contains an *ear* which you use to *hear* with. For example: *I hear he did well in his exam.*

- *Here* is a word about place. For example: *Have you come here to revise?*

To/too/two

- *To* means *towards* OR it can form part of a verb. For example: *it started to rain.*

- *Too* means *too much or also*. For example: *I've had too much cake/Would you like to come too?*

- *Two* means the number 2.

Its/it's

- *It's* is short for *it is* or *it has*. For example: *It's been a long term.*

- *Its* means *belonging to it*. For example: *The school celebrated its fifty-year anniversary.*

Practise/practice

- Practise is a verb. For example: *To be confident with spelling you must practise.*

- Practice is a noun. For example: *She works at a doctor's practice.*

Other words that are often confused

Other words sound *similar* and therefore are easily confused. For example:

were/where/wear · quite/quiet · effect/affect

are/our · advise/advice · accept/except · loose/lose

DO IT!

Write out a sentence for each of the following homophones:

- break/brake
- through/threw
- whether/weather
- passed/past.

CONTEXTUALISE IT!

The spelling mistakes in the piece of writing below make it quite difficult to read. This student makes lots of homophone mistakes, especially confusing the words their/there and are/our. Therefore, the student fails to spell with *reasonable accuracy in the context of the demands of the question* (Threshold performance) and would lose marks for the spelling part of their SPaG assessment.

> I'm greatful to live in a pieceful country were we don't have to worry about violence on the streets. Their our lots of reasons to feel safe. In the passed their where wars in this country, but now their is not so much unrest in the UK. We no that we our lucky to go too school and if we loose are job their our people to help.

Compound words

Compound words are created when two or more words are joined to make a new word. It is a common mistake to combine words that **should** be separate.

SNAP IT!

Compound words (one word)	together	himself	therefore	weekend	myself
	another	anyway	homemade	earthquake	anyone
Two separate words	a lot	a bit	all right	as well	all sorts

CHECK IT!

1 Give examples of two types of spelling mistake that a spellchecker might miss.

2 Look at the following list of spellings. Which parts of the words may be problematic? Which spelling rules and practical strategies might be useful when trying to remember these words? Practise remembering this list of spellings using various strategies and then reflect on which approaches worked well.

- usually
- occasion
- centre
- especially
- valuable
- together
- February

3 Which description of spelling accuracy gets the highest mark?

consistent accuracy   *reasonable accuracy*   *considerable accuracy*

Spelling: English literature

Introduction and advice

Using specialist words in your exam is important and, used correctly, will improve your marks. Specialist terms allow your writing to become more precise; your ideas will be focused and less generalised. Specialist words may not be part of your everyday language, so you may find them more difficult to spell and use.

Specialist terms

Here are some specialist words used in GCSE English literature, divided into helpful groups. Remember that many of these words will be used in more than one exam (for example, you might write about metaphors in your poetry, prose or drama exam).

Poetry		Prose fiction	
metaphor	stanza	character	repetition
simile	enjambment	narrative	protagonist
alliteration	sonnet	chapter	foreshadow
personification	figurative	structure	genre
rhyme	imagery	language	irony
rhythm	sibilance	theme	atmosphere
assonance	repetition	imagery	
Drama			
soliloquy		dialogue	
dramatic irony		monologue	
symbolism		playwright	
tragedy		Shakespeare	
scene		audience	

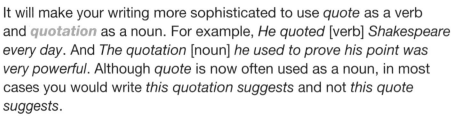

It will make your writing more sophisticated to use *quote* as a verb and *quotation* as a noun. For example, *He quoted* [verb] *Shakespeare every day*. And *The quotation* [noun] *he used to prove his point was very powerful*. Although *quote* is now often used as a noun, in most cases you would write *this quotation suggests* and not *this quote suggests*.

Don't just spot features in your writing. Instead weave the specialist terms into your argument. Focus on the **effects** of a feature, rather than just naming the feature. For example:

The writer uses a metaphor in the second stanza. ✗

The startling metaphor in the second stanza shocks the reader with its physical violence. ✔

CONTEXTUALISE IT!

The extract below from an essay shows a student using a wide range of specialist terms when answering a question about Shakespeare's play *Macbeth*. The terms are woven into the points and give the answer more **precision**. For example, the references to the **audience** show that the candidate understands the importance of the text as a performance. They use the specialist terms like irony **adeptly** – in other words they show a high level of skill.

The student would meet the High performance criteria for spelling: *Where required, they use a wide range of specialist terms **adeptly** and with **precision**.*

> The (audience) feels a strong sense of (irony) in Act 5, Scene 1 when Lady Macbeth frantically tries to remove an imagined blood stain from her hand. This (scene) reminds the (audience) of how much Lady Macbeth's (character) has changed. In Act 1 she believed a '…little water clears us of this deed…' but now the blood stain (symbolises) the depth of her guilt and anguish. Despite her earlier ruthlessness, Shakespeare now develops the more (tragic) elements of her (character) through her descent into madness.

NAIL IT!

In your English literature exam, it is important to spell a character's name correctly especially if the name appears on the exam paper. Identify any tricky characters' names in your exam texts and practise them.

Useful essay terms

The following words are also frequently used in English literature essays:

- quotation
- literature
- author
- quote
- novel
- development
- extract
- effect
- implied
- argument
- reader

STRETCH IT!

You might imagine that the word playwright would be spelled playwrite. It helps to use **etymology** to understand this unusual word.

The word playwright is not actually connected to writing. In Shakespeare's time, a wheelwright was someone who made wheels and a shipwright was someone who built ships. (The word *wright* means maker or builder.) Therefore, a playwright is someone who makes or builds plays!

Some other useful etymology:

soliloquy	From the Latin *solus* for *alone* and *loqui* for *speak*.
protagonist	From the Greek *protos* for first and *agonistes* for actor or competitor.
enjambment	From the French for *stride over*.
simile	From a Latin word meaning *like*.
sonnet	From Italian, meaning *little song*.

Spelling: Geography

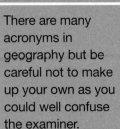
Introduction and advice

You are expected to learn many new words when you study geography. As the subject is about the world, some of these words come from different places which can make their spelling confusing. For example, we have borrowed the Japanese word *tsunami* (pronounced soo-nar-me) which literally translates as 'harbour wave'. Adding new geographical terms to your vocabulary can feel as if you're learning a new language, but with practice you will be spelling like a professional geographer.

Acronyms

Acronyms are used by geographers all the time and need to be spelled correctly. They enable you to simplify longer, commonly used phrases, saving time in the exam. In your exam always be careful to write out the phrase in full when you first use it, after this you can use the acronym.

Common phrases used in human geography	Acronym
Advanced Country	AC
Area of Outstanding Natural Beauty	AONB
Emerging Developing Country	EDC
Gross Domestic Product	GDP
Gross National Income	GNI
Gross National Product	GNP
Human Development Index	HDI
Lower Income Developing Country	LIDC
multinational company	MNC
non-governmental organisation	NGO

Commonly misspelled words in geography

There are certain words that are often misspelled in geography exams. Learning to spell these words correctly will mean you are making a positive impression from the start.

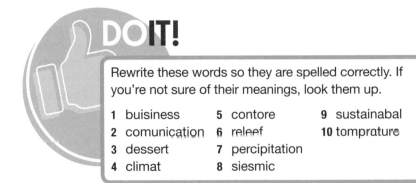

DO IT!

Rewrite these words so they are spelled correctly. If you're not sure of their meanings, look them up.

1 buisiness
2 comunication
3 dessert
4 climat
5 contore
6 releef
7 percipitation
8 siesmic
9 sustainabal
10 tomprature

Improving your vocabulary

The table below suggests ways of improving your geographical phrases.

What you are trying to say	Try using these words instead
plants and animals	flora and fauna
affecting people	having social implications
charities	NGOs
to make it last	to make it sustainable
rain	precipitation
planting trees	afforestation
cutting down trees	deforestation

Tricky plurals

A few words in geography can catch you out when you're trying to spell them as plurals. Review the rules from page 10 to remind yourself.

Place names

Spelling can make a significant difference to the quality of your written work. Look at this example of a student's piece of writing. The number of spelling mistakes mean they lose important marks.

CONTEXTUALISE IT!

The <u>Bosscasul</u> <u>fluds</u> <u>devistated</u> a small Cornish fishing <u>villege</u> in 2004. After an unprecedented amount off <u>percipitation</u> fell, the water level <u>rows</u> quickly because the village lay at the <u>conflooence</u> of the <u>to</u> rivers; Jordan and <u>Valensee</u>. The rescue efforts <u>where</u> excellent; <u>Severn</u> helicopters were <u>bought</u> in <u>too</u> rescue people off <u>rooves</u>. Because of the quick response by the emergency services, the <u>deth</u> <u>tole</u> was zero and the injury <u>tole</u> was one. A man broke his <u>thum</u>.

Although the content is correct and the candidate has tried to use a good range of specialist terms, the spelling mistakes mean that this example has only reached the Threshold performance level (*Candidates spell… with reasonable accuracy in the context of the demands of the question*). Place names (Boscastle/Valency) and key geographical terminology (confluence, precipitation) are spelled incorrectly. The student also makes homophone mistakes confusing to/too/two, rows/rose and where/were. There are also a number of other misspelled words including words repeated but spelled differently (villege and village).

NAIL IT!

Most exam boards ask you to look at geographical case studies or 'real world contexts' about specific places, so it is important that you learn to spell your place names correctly.

Turn these into plurals:

1 volcano
2 business
3 economy
4 country
5 city
6 county
7 valley
8 reef

Rewrite the exam answer, correcting all of the spelling mistakes.

Spelling: History

Introduction and advice

Part of your history exam will involve the use of sources. Sources are pieces of evidence from the past and could include letters, diary entries, speeches, posters or cartoons.

There are also specialist terms that you will need to use when looking at, and discussing, sources. These terms will help make your work stand out to an examiner. They can seem difficult to use, but if they appear in the question it is very important that you understand what they mean and know how to use them and spell them correctly in your answer.

The table below gives some key words you can use when discussing sources, along with their definitions.

Key words	Definitions
attribution	Who wrote the source and when
context	The events or background of the source
valid	Accurate or correct
utility	How useful it is
biased	Prejudiced for or against something
interpretation	An opinion
hindsight	Looking back at something
accuracy	How correct it is
reliable	How much you can trust it

NAIL IT!

If one of the key source words appears in the exam question, make sure you use it in your answer.

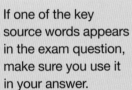

DO IT!

Create your own sentences similar to the ones above but with direct reference to the topics you are studying. Make sure you refer to the content in the modules from your exams

Using the words above will demonstrate that you can analyse a source effectively and will help you achieve the top marks on your source questions. They may seem tricky but when you see them in a sentence, they become easier to understand. For example:

- This source is clearly *biased*, as the author is giving a very one-sided account.

- As the source is written by a historian, they have the benefit of *hindsight* to see an overview of the events.

- This *interpretation* is clearly supported by my own knowledge of the topic.

- This source is valid as it gives *accurate* information.

- As the source is written by a historian, it is more *reliable* as they will have researched the information.

- The *context* of this source supports the argument, as it was written at the time of the event.

- The *attributions* of this source make it reliable, as it was written by someone at the time.

24

Specialist terminology

Within history there are many words that are unique to the subject. Some of these words are common across the whole subject, such as **chronology** or **parliament** and some are even more specialist and are only relevant to the topic you are studying, such as **medieval** or **soldier**.

The most difficult terms are often foreign words such as **Reichstag** or **Politburo** and for these words you need to know what they mean as well as how to spell them.

SUPPORT IT!

If the words use accents or umlauts (as in the ü in Führer), use them to help you remember how to spell them. For example, **détente** makes the **e** sound like **ay**: d**ay**tente. If you sound out the word in your head it will help you remember the spelling.

DO IT!

Go through your exercise books and write out any foreign words that come up in your topic. Write these on flash cards and on the back put the definition for the words. For example, **Führer = Leader (Adolf Hitler was Führer)**

Common spelling mistakes

armistice	feud	parliament
capitalism	foreign	political
century	government	refugee
centralisation	heir	reign
chronology	hierarchy	religious
colony	literacy	soldier
economy	medieval	weapons

These are only a small sample of words that are often misspelled. It is important to find the words that are common to the topics you study. You can do this by asking your teacher for a list of key words for each of your exam board modules.

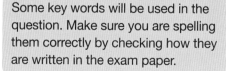

NAIL IT!

Some key words will be used in the question. Make sure you are spelling them correctly by checking how they are written in the exam paper.

DO IT!

Below is a selection of sentences with at least one word spelled incorrectly. Highlight the words that are incorrectly spelled and write out the correct spelling.

1 The goverment had a policy of centralistion.
2 The rein of Henry VIII was marked by forign wars and politicl problems.
3 Soliders were using wepons that were provided by the United States.
4 A system of hierachy existed in the country during the medival times.

Spelling: Religious studies

Introduction and advice

Religious studies uses many specific terms and key words that you need to know and use correctly.

It is important that you use the correct word when discussing particular religions because it shows that you understand that there are distinct differences between the religions that you have studied.

Sometimes the same word can have different meanings within different denominations (or branches) of the same religion. This can be a challenge but, with practice, specific terms will become more familiar.

Common misspellings

The words below are probably the most common words you will write in religious studies and they are frequently misspelled. Getting these common words correct, will help you avoid losing valuable marks.

belief	believe	religions
beliefs	religion	religious

Look at page 11 to revise the 'i before e (except after c)' rule. Note that the words 'theist', 'monotheist' and 'Atheist' don't follow the rule.

Attributes of God

Many people including Christians, Muslims and Jews believe in a God that is all-powerful, all-loving and all-knowing. These attributes have philosophical words linked to them. If you learn them and use them correctly, it will set you apart from other students. Philosophy means 'love of wisdom' (philo = ancient Greek for 'love'). A philosophical word is considered 'specialist terminology' which is credited within the SPaG marks.

DO IT!

Create flash cards with the attribute of God on one side and a picture to help you remember the word on the other side. Remember to spell the attributes correctly!

SNAP IT!

Attribute of God	Meaning	Comment
omniscient	all-knowing	*Omni* is a Latin **prefix** meaning *all*. Watch the 'ie' combination in omniscient as it doesn't follow the rule!
omni-benevolent	all-loving	
omnipotent	all-powerful	
omnipresent	present everywhere, always	
monotheistic	there is only one God	*Mono* is a Greek prefix meaning *one*.

Christianity *-ion* words

There are lots of words within Christianity that end in *-ion* because they come from Latin words. They generally mean an action or a condition.

 SUPPORT IT!

> If there is a 't' or 'te' at the end of the root word use *-tion* (for example, incarnate → incarnation). If there is a 'd', 'de' or 'se' at the end of the root word use *-sion* (for example, intercede → intercession).

Non-English words

Many words that you have to learn are not English. Practise writing these or spelling them out loud.

In some religions, such as Buddhism, there may be more than one accepted spelling for a word (for example, the word *karma* in Sanskrit is spelled *kamma* in Pali). Keep to one language for all your spellings, and use the same spelling each time you use a word in an answer.

It is also important that you use the correct word when discussing different religions. For example, you should refer to a synagogue, not a Jewish church.

Similar, but different

Many words used in religious studies look and sound similar to others but are, in fact, very different from each other. Make sure you don't get them mixed up as it will make your writing confusing.

angel: a spiritual being believed to act as an attendant, agent, or messenger of God.

angle: a corner, usually measured in degrees.

conscience: the voice in our heads that tell us what is right and wrong.
conscious (consciousness): the sense of being awake or aware.

contraception: a method to prevent pregnancy.
conception: the moment where the egg is fertilised by the sperm.

father: a male parent or a title given to a priest. Also used as a name for God. Part of the Trinity.
farther: over a long distance.

practise (verb): to perform an activity regularly (for example, in some countries people are not free to practise their religious beliefs.)
practice (noun): the repeated performance of an activity (for example, the Islamic practice of Wudu – washing).

sacred: connected with religion.
scared: frightened.

DO IT!

Complete these words with the correct endings. If you are not sure what they mean, look them up!

1 revela _____
2 crucifix _____
3 ascen _____
4 denomina _____
5 confes _____
6 medita _____

DO IT!

Write out sentences that use the words to the right in context to help you remember them.

Punctuation essentials

Introduction and advice

Punctuation marks help you create meaning in your writing, just as hand gestures, tone of voice and facial expressions help create meaning when you speak. However, even very experienced writers sometimes face difficulties with their punctuation.

If you lack confidence with punctuation, you may find that you are using fewer punctuation marks in your writing and even avoiding some punctuation marks altogether.

Why is accurate punctuation important?

- Punctuation makes your writing clearer.
- When used accurately, punctuation marks give you more control over your meaning and tone.
- A punctuation mark in the **wrong** place can change the whole meaning of your writing.
- If you use accurate punctuation, you will pick up more marks in some of your exam.

> *"….all our thoughts can be rendered with absolute clarity if we bother to put the right dots and squiggles between the words in the right places. Proper punctuation is both the sign and the cause of clear thinking."* (Lynne Truss, author of 'Eats, Shoots & Leaves')

Grammar checkers

Just as spell checkers can be unreliable, grammar checkers can sometimes highlight mistakes that are not there. Grammar checks may also miss an inaccurate use of punctuation. It is much better to understand how to use punctuation correctly, so you don't need to trust in the grammar checker to spot your mistakes. You also can't use a grammar checker in your exam!

SUPPORT IT!

Make sure you know what each punctuation mark looks like:

.	Full stop	–	Dash
,	Comma	-	Hyphen
;	Semi-colon	" " or ' '	Speech marks/ quotation marks/ inverted commas
:	Colon		
( )	Brackets	…	Ellipsis

DO IT!

Which punctuation marks do you use every day in your writing? Are there any punctuation marks that you avoid because you don't know how to use them correctly?

Punctuation to end a sentence

Most of the time, you will use a **full stop** to signal that a sentence has ended.

However, **question marks** and **exclamation marks** might also be used **instead** of a full stop. A question mark is used to signal that you are asking a question and an exclamation mark signals surprise or a strong emotion.

- *Shakespeare's plays present a range of complex characters.*

- *Why do Shakespeare's plays present such a range of complex characters?*

- *Shakespeare's characters are complex!*

NAIL IT!

Some writers overuse exclamation marks. It is better to avoid this punctuation mark in formal exam answers. If you really need to use an exclamation mark, never use more than one.

CONTEXTUALISE IT!

A common mistake is to allow sentences to 'run-on' without any punctuation to signal the end of each sentence. When you are under pressure in an exam, you are more likely to make this mistake.

For example:

> San Francisco suffered a devastating earthquake in 1906 that destroyed the majority of the city's buildings and was followed by a massive fire that caused even more devastation and left thousands of the city's inhabitants homeless and watching in horror as their city was destroyed.

This 'run-on' sentence is difficult to read and needs rewording so that the end of each sentence is clearly marked.

For example: Add in two full stops and remove a few **conjunctions** (like the word **and**) to make these sentences much easier to read. Understanding and revising a range of punctuation marks will help you avoid 'run-on' sentences.

NAIL IT!

At the end of a sentence, never use a question mark **and** a full stop. The question mark replaces the full stop to signal the end of a sentence.

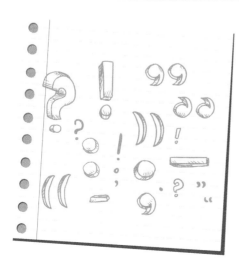

Capital letters

Capital letters are useful signals for the reader. The most common reason to use one is to show the reader that you are starting a new sentence. For example: *The play opens with the Birling family having a dinner party.*

Capital letters also have other roles:

- To signal a proper noun (a name of a person, or the name of a place, or a country, like George, Scunthorpe, Africa).

- To signal an official title (like Mrs, Mr or Doctor).

- To show important words in a title (like Main Religions of the World). Avoid using capitals for less important words in a title: *of, and*.

- To show the name of special days of the year (like Easter, Eid or Diwali).

- They show important words in the titles of books, films and organisations (for example, Leeds University, or 'Pride and Prejudice').

- When using the first letter of an abbreviated word (for example in geography, LIDC would stand for Lower Income Developing Country).

NAIL IT!

It is essential that all formal texts use capital letters correctly.

DO IT!

Rewrite this exam answer, adding in capital letters and full stops and removing any unwanted capital letters. (There are 17 mistakes to find.)

CONTEXTUALISE IT!

This extract from an exam answer is difficult to read because there are no capital letters or full stops. The student has failed to use capital letters to indicate the characters' names and has added some capitals where they are not needed.

> bob cratchit is presented to the reader in a Sympathetic way, as we are encouraged to pity the character scrooge, by contrast, represents those members of the Upper Classes who Shut themselves off from the rest of the community in order to feel glad at the end of the Story, the readers need to dislike him at the start cratchit is a Symbol of the moral poor scrooge is a symbol of the greedy rich

The mistakes in this piece of writing affect its meaning, so the student would not be awarded any marks for this part of the SPaG assessment as *Errors severely hinder the meaning of the response.*

How to use commas accurately

Commas are the most frequently used punctuation mark, but they may also be the most challenging to use. The inaccurate use of a comma can confuse your reader or even give your writing a different meaning.

Commas are tricky because they can do lots of different jobs within a sentence.

1 The most important function of a comma is to divide two points.

Let's eat Grandpa.

Let's eat, Grandpa.

Commas save lives.

- *Phoebe had a religious studies exam in the morning,* **so** *the history revision would have to wait.*

- *She was confident about her science exam,* **but** *still had some issues with geography.*

These two points are divided by a comma **and** linked by the conjunction.

It would be incorrect to use a comma in the following sentence:

- *She revised her prose texts, she re-read the first act of Romeo and Juliet.* **X**

These two sentences could be separated by a full stop **or** you could add a conjunction to the comma to link the two sentences.

- *She revised her prose texts, and she re-read the first act of Romeo and Juliet.* ✔

The comma here signals that the sentence is continuing.

2 Commas can also be used to separate introductory words, longer linking words or phrases at the start of a sentence.

- *However, she was aware that there were significant gaps in her revision notes.*

- *In conclusion, Lady Macbeth changes significantly since her first appearance in Act one.*

- *Nevertheless, plastic pollution remains an important issue for the world community.*

3 Commas can also be used to separate extra information within a sentence.

- *He revised history, his most challenging subject, in the afternoon.*

- *She didn't want to socialise during her study leave, which caused a problem with some of her friends.*

The extra information could appear at the start of a sentence, at the end or within the sentence. All of these sentences would still work without the extra information.

④ Commas are also useful when you need to separate three or more items within a list.

- *He gathered together his notes, exercise books, exam texts and highlighters.*

- *She had to revise erosion, natural hazards, coastal landscapes and world economics.*

SUPPORT IT!

Remember to use 'and' to separate the last two items in a list.

STRETCH IT!

The Oxford comma (sometimes called the serial comma) is when a comma is added in a list before the 'and'. Not everyone agrees that this comma is needed and generally in the UK it is not used.

CONTEXTUALISE IT!

It is important to remember that too many commas in the wrong place can also affect the clarity of your writing:

> He was revising, very hard and worked, all evening, to complete, his revision. His family, were supportive, and tried, to be, very quiet around the house and, sometimes, his little sister, would disturb him, his parents, bought him some useful, equipment like post-it notes, highlighters and folders, to organise his notes.

The use of commas in this example makes the writing very fragmented and distracts from the meaning of the sentences. The second sentence is too long and should contain a full stop instead of a comma after *disturb him*. The overuse of commas would lose marks in the SPaG assessment.

"PEOPLE JUST DON'T UNDERSTAND ME!"

SNAP IT!

DON'T use a comma…

- **…between adverbs and adjectives:**

My desk is a horribly chaotic mess of revision notes and scrap paper. ✔
My desk is a horribly, chaotic mess of revision notes and scrap paper. ✗

- **…between adjectives and nouns:**

She was a confident writer of essays. ✔
She was a confident, writer of essays. ✗

- **…before the first item or the last item in a list:**

He decided that his French, history and geography notes needed more detail. ✔
He decided that his, French, history and geography, notes needed more detail. ✗

How to use semicolons

Used correctly, a semicolon can make your writing more sophisticated.

There are two main reasons to use a semicolon. You will probably use the first reason more frequently.

1 To join two closely connected ideas.

- *I can't go out tonight; I have my GCSE history exam tomorrow.*

- *In Act One Lady Macbeth is presented as a powerful character; in Act Five she has lost her power over Macbeth and herself.*

Each of these two examples is one long sentence. The semicolon has joined together two smaller sentences that have closely connected ideas. A full stop could have been used (making the two ideas more separate) but a semicolon is more effective because it links ideas.

2 To break up a list that contains longer phrases.

- *When you are revising, make sure you have somewhere quiet to study; gather together all your notes from class; make a revision plan, with breaks; focus on what you are revising, rather than worrying about what you haven't covered.*

The semicolon organises this list into clear sections and shows that the ideas are connected. Using just commas would make the list too confusing.

Which of these sentences use semi-colons correctly? Tick or cross each sentence.

1 The main tourist attractions in London; are the London eye on the south bank; of the river Thames; the tower of London on the north bank; of the River Thames Trafalgar Square and Buckingham Palace in the City of Westminster.

2 James I was very interested in witchcraft; Shakespeare wanted to use the play 'Macbeth' to flatter the king.

3 Muslims believe that Muhammed; was the last prophet sent by Allah prophets were sent; to mankind to teach them how to live.

NAIL IT!

A semi-colon can often replace the word 'and' to join two sentences of equal importance.

Avoid a semi-colon if one of the sections does not make sense on its own:

- *Although it was tiring; she carried on her revision.* ✗

- *Although it was tiring, she carried on her revision.* ✔

STRETCH IT!

Some writers use a **dash** instead of a semi-colon. When might a dash be unsuitable? Read more about dashes on page 37.

NAIL IT!

It is sometimes useful to think about the colon as the drum roll before the revealing of an idea.

How to use colons

There are three main reasons for using a **colon**.

1 **To introduce an idea**

- *Mary's life was full of dramatic events: at just six days old she became Queen of Scotland.*

2 **To introduce a list**

- *There are three main themes in 'The Merchant of Venice': mercy, idealism and prejudice.*

3 **To introduce a quotation**

- *The seven deadly sins are dealt with in the Bible, including the sin of envy: 'A sound heart is life to the body, but envy is rottenness to the bones.'*

NAIL IT!

Don't confuse semi-colons and colons. Mixing up these two punctuation marks can change the whole meaning of a sentence. For example:

- *Ralph was terrified; Jack was out of control.*

This use of a semi-colon here suggests the two ideas are linked.

- *Ralph was terrified: Jack was out of control.*

The use of a colon here shows that Ralph was terrified **because** Jack was out of control.

CONTEXTUALISE IT!

This extract uses a range of punctuation accurately and effectively. The use of the colon in the first sentence is effective. The student shows *consistent accuracy and effective control of meaning* (High performance).

Effective use of a colon to introduce a short list

> Romeo can be described in two words: romantic and impetuous. Although he does have his faults, his passion makes him a very likeable character. The audience first meets Romeo after the street fighting in Act 1. At the start of the play he is presented as a lovesick character who laments his unrequited love for Rosaline.

DO IT!

Add a colon in the correct place to each of the following sentences:

1 When analysing poetry, it is important to focus on three main areas language, form and structure.

2 Chalk is a permeable rock it lets water through.

How to use brackets

Brackets are useful because they enclose and separate extra information within a sentence, for example, a date, definition or a short explanation. This means you can add more to the sentence without disturbing the main idea.

- *Elizabeth I (1558–1603) was a powerful and popular monarch.*
- *Elizabeth I (who reigned from 1558–1603) was a powerful and popular monarch.*
- *Elizabeth I was a powerful and popular monarch (a person who reigns over a kingdom).*

When the brackets appear at the end of a sentence, the full stop is always outside the final bracket. To check if you have used brackets correctly, remove the bracketed information to see if the remaining sentence still makes sense.

It is useful to remember that many brackets act in a similar way to a pair of commas, separating extra information within the sentence.

- *Elizabeth I, who reigned from 1558–1603, was a powerful and popular monarch.*

STRETCH IT!

Square brackets [ ] have various functions and are normally used by someone adding extra information after the original writer.

Curly brackets or braces {} are normally only used by specialists in programming, music annotation or scientific writing. Neither of these types of brackets are suitable for a handwritten exam answer, so don't use them in your writing.

DO IT!

Add one pair of brackets to each of the following sentences:

1 The First World War 1914–18 drew in all the world's powerful countries.
2 Earthquakes are detected by seismographs electromagnetic sensors that translate ground motions into electrical changes.
3 In the Jewish religion, the most important day of the week is Shabbat the Sabbath.

(Brackets always come in pairs. Remember to close your brackets!)

How to use hyphens

Hyphens are used to join whole words or parts of words together. They can be tricky to use and a mistake with a hyphen could lead to a spelling mistake or a lack of clarity.

Some compound words use hyphens:

> mother-in-law make-up runner-up
>
> counter-attack vice-president

Compound numbers and fractions also use a hyphen:

> seventy-two three-fifths
>
> twenty-one one-eighth

Sometimes a hyphen is used to create a compound **adjective** before a noun:

> rock-forming minerals free-range eggs
>
> two-year-old cat up-to-date research

Sometimes hyphens are used to connect a prefix to the main word. You usually need a prefix hyphen for the following reasons:

- In history, to separate the prefix from a date or name, for example, *pre-1900, post-Victorian*.

- To avoid confusion with another word, for example, *re-cover* (to make a clear difference to the word *recover*), *re-form* (to make a clear difference to the word reform)

- If the prefix ends with a vowel and the main word begins with a vowel, a hyphen is usually needed, for example, *co-owned, pre-eminent*.

SUPPORT**IT!**

A compound word is when two or more words are combined to make a new word. A compound adjective is formed when two words are connected with a hyphen to create an adjective.

STRETCH**IT!**

Hyphenated words are becoming less common (for example, the word e-mail is often now written as email).

SUPPORT**IT!**

A hyphen looks similar to a dash (but a dash is longer). A dash has a different function in a sentence, so don't confuse the two. Learn more about the dash on the next page.

- *Molly Kenzie (the only girl I ever loved) had just arrived at the party.*
- *Molly Kenzie, the only girl I ever loved, had just arrived at the party.*

The use of the dash here gives emphasis to the phrase *the only girl I ever loved*. This effect is not achieved by the use of brackets or commas.

Fiction writers may also use the dash to create a sense of tension in their writing, for example: *The house appeared to be empty – but was it?*

Using quotation marks

In some exam answers, you will need to select a short piece of a text to support your argument. This is called a quotation. It is important to use the correct punctuation when using a quotation.

The main punctuation marks used in a quotation are **quotation marks** (or speech marks).

The rules for using them are straightforward:

1 The quotation marks go around the words you are copying from the text:

   Macbeth is not sure if the dagger is real or a vision prompted by his guilt: 'Is this a dagger I see before me?'

2 The quotation can end with either a comma, full stop, exclamation mark or question mark. If these punctuation marks are part of the quotation, they go **inside** the second set of speech marks.

   - *Lady Macbeth shows her guilty state of mind: 'Out damn spot! Out I say!'* ✔
   - *Lady Macbeth shows her guilty state of mind: 'Out damn spot! Out I say'!* ✗

3 You can either embed a short quotation in a sentence or use a colon to separate a longer quotation from your point.

   - *Macbeth's 'vaulting ambition' is prompting him to kill the king.*
   - *Macbeth is at first reluctant to kill the king, but his ambition drives his decision: '…only vaulting ambition, which o'erleaps itself…'*

4 Always use the punctuation used in the original text. If the quotation is only a section of a sentence, you can use **ellipsis** (the three dots to show words are missing) to suggest there was more before and after the quotation. See page 38 to read more about ellipsis.

NAILIT!

The dash should usually be avoided in formal writing, so avoid it in your exam.

NAILIT!

If the text you are quoting from appears in your exam, make sure you copy out the exact words in your quotation.

SUPPORTIT!

Never use long quotations in your exam answer. Be selective and keep it short.

Ellipses

An ellipsis is shown by three dots (…). It indicates that part of a sentence is missing. Sometimes fiction writers also use an ellipsis to show tension or anticipation:

- *The door opened…*

Most of the time these marks are not appropriate in formal writing. The main reason for using an ellipsis in an exam is to show that part of a sentence is missing in a quotation:

- *The writer chooses vocabulary that suggests an atmosphere of unease: '…shivering… glanced…hesitating…'*

The ellipses show the examiner that these words have been picked from different parts of the original text.

How to use apostrophes

Apostrophes are one of the trickiest forms of punctuation to use correctly. There are two types of apostrophe: apostrophes to show contraction and apostrophes to show possession.

Apostrophes to show contraction

A contraction is a shortened form of a phrase. An apostrophe signals that some letters are missing. In **don't**, the apostrophe signals that the 'o' has been removed from this shortened version of **do not**.

Here are some common contractions:

SNAP IT!

Original form	Contraction
would have	would've
could have	could've
should have	should've
they are	they're
who is	who's
are not	aren't
do not	don't
does not	doesn't
cannot	can't
is not	isn't
I am	I'm
I will	I'll
she will	she'll
I would	I'd
they would	they'd
I had	I'd
I have	I've

"More might have turned up, Sir, if you had put the apostrophe in the correct place…"

There are also irregular contractions. For example:

- *Many students will not (won't) have a quiet place to study at home.*

In this example, the first letters of the contraction *won't* do not follow the same letter sequence as *will not*. However, the apostrophe is still used between the 'n' and the 't' to suggest that the 'o' has been removed.

STRETCHIT!

A few other words in our language **only** use the shortened form, because the longer form is no longer used. For example:

o'clock = of the clock

NAILIT!

Most contractions should be avoided in formal writing.

SUPPORTIT!

Remember that the apostrophe is usually placed where the letters are missing. It is a common mistake to place the apostrophe in the wrong place:

✔ couldn't = the apostrophe shows that the letter 'o' is missing from *could not*.

✗ could'nt = this apostrophe has been added in the wrong place

Apostrophes to show possession

Possessive apostrophes signal to the reader that something belongs to someone or something:

- *The revision notes were on Sam's desk.*

In the phrase *Sam's desk* the apostrophe is **not** showing that a letter is missing. Instead the added apostrophe and the 's' are signalling to the reader that the desk *belongs* to Sam.

If a name is singular and ends in 's', add 's' unless the last syllable of the name is pronounced 'iz', for example:

- *The revision notes were on Ross's desk.*
- *Moses' ten commandments were given on Mount Sinai.*

However, if a plural word ends in an 's', you just add an apostrophe:

- *The revision notes were placed on the students' desks.*

In this sentence, because there is more than one student (plural) the apostrophe is added **after** the 's'.

If the plural word **doesn't** end in an 's', then an apostrophe and an 's' can be added:

- The revision notes were placed on the children's desks.

Misuse of apostrophes

Do not overuse apostrophes!

1 **Never** use an apostrophe to turn a word into a plural, for example:

- *There have been many serious earthquake's in recent years.* ✗
- *There have been many serious earthquakes in recent years.* ✔

2 Many **pronouns** (like his, her, your, whose, their, its) don't use a possessive apostrophe. For example, never use a possessive apostrophe with the word *its*.

- *The cat cleaned its fur.* ✔
- *The cat cleaned it's fur.* ✗
- *The cat cleaned its' fur.* ✗

The contraction *it's* is only used for *it is* or *it has*.

3 Verbs don't have apostrophes (only nouns have them), so be careful not to add an apostrophe to verbs ending in an 's':

- *She see's the importance of starting revision early.* ✗
- *She sees the importance of starting revision early.* ✔

CHECKIT!

1 Give two reasons why accurate punctuation is important.

2 The following exam answer has accurate punctuation, but a greater *variety* of punctuation could be used to improve the fluency and effectiveness of the writing. Experiment with different ways of rewriting this paragraph (for example, using punctuation to join shorter sentences or using punctuation to replace a conjunction).

> Mr Birling is an important character. He is the head of the Birling family. He dominates the first part of the play with long speeches. The content of these speeches shows he is out of touch with society. He is presented as a pompous and over confident and selfish character.

3 Create a revision poster containing all the different types of punctuation. Include definitions, uses and your own examples.

4 When should an ellipsis be used?

a When you've run out of things to say in an exam.

b To signal that part of the sentence is missing in a quotation.

c To signal the end of a sentence.

5 Find one of your long exam essays. Pick two paragraphs from the essay and rewrite them, changing the punctuation to improve the clarity of the sentences. Experiment with using punctuation marks for effect, rather than just accuracy.

Punctuation: English literature

Introduction and advice

Using the correct capital letters and punctuation marks in your English literature exam will help you pick up more marks for your SPaG assessment. Writing an English literature essay also requires some specialist punctuation.

Capital letters

It is important to remember which key words have capital letters. It is a common mistake to forget that characters' first names and surnames **always** have a capital letter. For example: Beatrice, Duncan, Mr Darcy, Dr Jekyll, Lady Macbeth.

The name of the writer also has capital letters: Robert Louis Stevenson, William Shakespeare, Jane Austen, Sir Arthur Conan Doyle.

The first time you refer to the writer, use their full name. After that you can just use their surname. The only exception to this is when you are writing about Shakespeare, when it is acceptable to always just use the playwright's surname. Never refer to a writer by their first name only!

It is also important to use capitals to signal the title of your text. Only the main words are given a capital letter in a title. For example:

- 'Romeo and Juliet'
- 'The Strange Case of Dr Jekyll and Mr Hyde'
- 'The Sign of Four'
- 'Pride and Prejudice'
- 'A Christmas Carol'

Small linking words such as **and**, **of** and **the** are not given capital letters unless they are the first word in the title.

NAILIT!

It is acceptable to shorten a very long title in your exam. For example, it is acceptable to shorten 'The Strange Case of Dr Jekyll and Mr Hyde' to 'Dr Jekyll and Mr Hyde' or even 'Jekyll and Hyde'. However, never shorten titles to abbreviations such as 'P&P' instead of 'Pride and Prejudice'.

DOIT!

Look carefully through your exercise books and see if you can spot any capital letter mistakes. Can you spot a pattern in your mistakes? Are there any characters' names you use regularly, where you frequently forget the capital letter?

SUPPORTIT!

Don't forget to use a capital letter for Shakespeare! Using a lower case 's' is a very common mistake and will be noticed by the examiner.

The words **author**, **writer** and **playwright** do not have capital letters.

Quotation marks

You can use **either** single **or** double quotation marks to signal you are using a quotation.

They are also used to signal the title of a play, novel or poem. It is particularly important to use this signal when the play is named after a main character. For example:

- Macbeth is full of tragedy.
- 'Macbeth' is full of tragedy.

The second example indicates that the **play** is being written about; the first example suggests the **character** of Macbeth is the focus.

Drama quotations

You may want to include some information to show where your quotation comes from. **This is not compulsory**, especially as you won't have a copy of your play in the exam. However, if you do decide to include this information, you must use the correct layout.

> Lady Macbeth's language starts to reveal her feelings of guilt: 'The Thane of Fife had a wife.' (Act Five, scene one) **or** (5.1).

DO IT!

Rewrite the following sentences, correcting any mistakes.

1 In act 1 of "an inspector calls" the character of mr birling states that "The Germans don't want war. Nobody wants war…"
2 The Playwright focuses on the theme of class in act 2: the Narrator states that '…what we, the English, have come to know as class?"

The information in brackets in the example above shows where the quotation is from in the play. In the first example, the word **Act** has a capital and the word **scene** does not, the words are also separated by a comma. In the second example, only the Act number and scene number are used, separated by a full stop.

Alternatively, you may make this information part of the sentence:

In Act Five, scene one Lady Macbeth's language starts to reveal her feelings of guilt:
- *'The Thane of Fife had a wife.'*

You will notice that the word **Act** still has a capital letter and is separated from **scene** by a comma.

Shakespeare and contractions

In Shakespeare's time contractions were common. There are various shortened versions of words and phrases in the plays such as 'ne'er' for 'never' and 'e'en' for 'even'. When you copy a Shakespearian quotation containing a contraction, make sure you put the apostrophe in the correct place.

Punctuation: Geography

Introduction and advice

Some uses of punctuation, specific to geography, will help you to be successful on the SPaG elements of your exams.

Capital letters and place names

Always use a capital letter when you're referring to the name of a place, such as a city, county, country or region. If the place name has two or three words, they all need a capital letter: Oxford Street or Central African Republic. A capital letter is not needed for city, island or street unless they form part of a name: Atlantic City, Fraser Island, Prince's Street.

Prepositions in place names do not need capitals, for example, Ashton-under-Lyne. If a country name starts with 'the', that will need a capital too, for example, The Bahamas.

DO IT!

> Rewrite these examples to include any capital letters that might be missing. (Some might not need any capitals at all.)
>
> | | | |
> |---|---|---|
> | bristol | kingston upon thames | the ocean |
> | the park | new york city | the democratic republic of congo |
> | hollywood boulevard | a city | |
> | mumbai | pacific ocean | the river wye |

Points of the compass and place names

What about north, south, east and west? If the place name includes points of the compass, they must be capitalised too. If you're using compass directions in another context such as navigation, no capital letters are needed. For example, to get to **North** Queensferry you need to drive **north** along the M90.

SUPPORT IT!

Use this rhyme to help you remember:

Compass in the name? Play the capital game.

Compass in the route? Little letters are more cute.

Colons

Any list can follow a colon. For example, you might be listing the social, economic and environmental impacts of a natural hazard.

- *The earthquake caused the following social impacts: 17 deaths; 42 homes to collapse; 400 homes to lose power and the loss of 15 small businesses...*

Semicolons have been used because the list includes some longer phrases.

A colon can also be used to present a valid conclusion.

- *Longshore drift was evident: a spit formed at the end of headland.*

DO IT!

Identify three other potential topics where a colon and a list would be a useful addition to an answer.

SNAP IT!

- through-flow
- counter-urbanisation
- non-governmental organisations
- non-renewable energy
- hydro-electricity
- Sub-Saharan Africa (this has three capitals as it is a place name)
- freeze-thaw

Hyphens

The common words and phrases shown in the Snap It! box need hyphens. (Notice that the second word doesn't have a capital letter and the first only does if it is at the beginning of a sentence.)

Using brackets to enhance detail

Using brackets can add detail to your answers without a lot of additional writing. For example: 'Hurricanes only form above warm water (above 27°C)', or 'London's population density is high (above 5,200/km^2)'.

Quotations and fieldwork

All exam boards require you to complete fieldwork and collect primary data. When writing up your findings, it is useful to be able to quote specific responses to any questionnaires or surveys that you undertook. Remember to use quotation marks to show the exact words from the survey.

CONTEXTUALISE IT!

This student has used qualitative (descriptive) data to answer the question. This is highlighted by the use of speech marks. Quantitative (actual values) data would have also been appropriate for this answer but would not have required the use of speech marks.

On my fieldtrip to Lulworth 10 people completed my questionnaire about how long they were staying in the area and what they were doing there. Most people were visiting Lulworth for the day. One man responded: 'We've just driven down today, it's so beautiful here and the carpark is so big we can always find a space'. This helped me to understand that it's a honey pot site because of its natural beauty but also, it's attractive to visitors because the estate has been well managed. The provision of facilities for day trip visitors has been improved.

Apostrophes

In geography, all sorts of things such as cities, individuals, organisations and physical features may require an apostrophe to indicate possession.

DO IT!

Review the rules about apostrophes on pages 38 and 39 before rewriting these sentences to include an apostrophe to indicate possession.

1 The policies of the government aimed to reduce poverty.
2 Johannesburg has slum areas with high crime rates.
3 The eruption of the volcano had a devastating impact on the habitat of the local wildlife.

Punctuation: History

Key dates

Studying history involves knowing and using dates. It is important that you write dates accurately so they are clear to an examiner. There is a range of ways that you can layout dates. For example, if you are writing a range of dates you can put a dash between such as 1872–87 or you can write 1872 to 1887. If you are writing a word between them you need to write the full date; if it is a dash you can shorten it to just the last two numbers, as long as the century is the same.

Centuries

When you are discussing a date or time period in the exam, using the correct terminology is important. When you are writing about centuries, you can write the whole word out or you can abbreviate it to a 'C' before the date you have written, for example, C17. It must be a capital 'C' or you may get it confused with the word circa (see page 46). Getting the century correct is also important.

DO IT!

Look at the list below; when it gives a year write the correct century next to it (for example, 1873 = 19th century), and when it gives a century write a year in the century next to it (for example, 17th century = 1654).

1   20th century =
2   234 =
3   14th century =
4   1781 =
5   1398 =
6   467 =
7   17th century =
8   6th century =
9   1066 =
10 1555 =

SUPPORT IT!

If you ignore the last two numbers of any date and add 1 to whatever the first number (or first two numbers are) that will always get you to the correct century. So for the year 1743 for example, ignore the 43 and add 1 to 17 to make 18. So 1743 is therefore in the 18th century.

Your exam includes a thematic study of a period of over 1000 years. This means you need to know about time periods within that. However, some time periods have different labels. For example, the Middle Ages and Medieval times are different names for the same time period (approximately 1000 to 1500).

DO IT!

Put the correct labels next to the time periods given in the table. Remember, there will be at least two labels for the same time period.

Labels: Middle Ages, Industrial Age, Early Modern, Technological Age, Tudor, Victorian, Modern Age, 20th century, Medieval, Georgian

1000 – 1500	
1500 – 1700	
1700 – 1900	
1900 – present	

 ## SUPPORT IT!

You may see a date preceded by a 'c', for example, *c*1000. The 'c' stands for circa, which is a Latin word meaning 'around' and shows that there is no definite date for the time period but it is 'around' the date given.

Abbreviations and names

It is acceptable for you to use abbreviations in your written work. The most common abbreviations tend to refer to time periods.

- BCE generally means 'Before Common Era' and refers to before the year 0. It can also be written BC meaning 'Before Christ'.

- AD (Anno Domini) is the most recognised abbreviation for after the year 0 and means 'In the year of the Lord'. It can sometimes be seen as CE, which means 'Common Era'.

Capital letters

Capital letters are used at the start of sentences and for proper nouns. These include names, specific places, and things. It is vitally important to capitalise names of key people and all the words in the name of something; for example, in Weimar Republic both words must be capitalised.

DO IT!

Read through the passage below and add in all the capital letters that are missing

women during world war one worked hard in a range of industries. at the start of the war, the leader of the suffragettes, emmeline pankhurst, along with her daughter, christabel, called for an end to their campaigning in order to support the soldiers fighting in france and belgium. this led to women working in munitions factories as well as other industries to help support the front line. after the war, the home secretary, george cave, introduced the representation of the people act 1918 which, when passed, allowed some women the right to vote. only in 1928 did women gain equal terms with men.

Punctuation: Religious studies

Upper and lower case letters

SNAP IT!

The following ALWAYS need a capital letter	For example...	Comment
Names of people	Jesus, Muhammad (pbuh), Guru Nanak, Siddhartha Gautama, Buddha	This includes God or Brahman or Allah. They **must** have a capital letter.
Religions	Christianity, Hinduism, Islam, Sikhism, Judaism, Buddhism	Humanism is not considered a religion but more a 'non-religious belief set' so does not necessarily need a capital letter.
Religious groups and denominations	Muslims, Theravada Buddhists, Quakers, Roman Catholics	The followers of the religion Islam are called Muslims.
Holy books	The Bible, Qur'an, Torah, Hadith, Genesis, Dhammapada	Note where the apostrophe is in Qur'an.
Places	Jerusalem, Lourdes, Israel, Bodh Gaya and the river Ganges	
Festivals and holy days	Christmas, Easter, Wesak, Ramadan, baptism and confirmation	

Using quotations

To show you have an understanding of religious teachings and how these relate to modern practices you need to use quotations from holy books or religious people. Use quotation marks at the beginning and end of the quote. If you can, write where the quote can be found, for example:

- *In the Sermon on the Mount (also known as the Beatitudes), Jesus tells the crowds 'blessed are the peacemakers, for they will be called children of God.' (Matthew 5: 9). This is why many Christians are pacifist or against war and violence.*

SUPPORT IT!

Quotations don't have to be long. A few words will show the examiner that you can make links between religious ideas and the evidence behind them.

STRETCH IT!

Look through your exercise book and write down useful quotes that you can use in the exam.

DO IT!

Look at a Bible to find these quotations about relationships and family:

- Genesis 2: 22–24
- Matthew 19: 4–6
- Mark 10: 11–12
- Exodus 20: 14
- 1 Corinthians 7: 10–11

Bible verses

Bible verses start with the book that they are found in followed by the chapter, then a colon and then the verse (or verses (plural) separated by a dash).

For example, the first story of Creation (the six days of Creation) is found in the book of Genesis, chapter 1, verses 1 to 31 so it is written 'Genesis 1: 1–31'.

If you want to just quote one verse, such as, 'That is why a man leaves his father and mother and is united to his wife, and they become one flesh' then you can just use the verse reference 'Genesis 2: 24'.

Some books of the Bible have two parts (such as Chronicles in the Old Testament and Corinthians in the New Testament). These are written with the book number first, then name, chapter number, colon and the number of the verse(s). For example: '1 Corinthians 15: 12–58' or '1 Peter 2: 1–7'.

Apostrophes showing contraction

Could've, would've, should've

Many students think that the apostrophe in could've, would've and should've is hiding the word 'of', but it is 'have': *I could have gone out but instead I stayed home and revised*.

DO IT!

It is advisable not to use contractions in your exam. Expand the following sentences:

1 Siddhartha Gautama could've stayed in the palace all his life.
2 Christians should've done more to save the environment.
3 Malala Yusafzai would've still spoken out for girls' rights even if she had not been shot by the Taliban.

Apostrophes showing possession

Look at the following sentences to remind yourself of where apostrophes should be placed.

- Jesus' followers were called disciples.
- The Gospels' central theme is the life and teachings of Jesus.
- The Gurus' lives are retold in many Sikh stories.

NAIL IT!

Apostrophes matter! Using apostrophes correctly will gain you important SPaG marks and makes your writing clear. Many employers value good spelling, punctuation and grammar so it really is a skill for life.

Grammar essentials

Introduction and advice

Grammar focuses on the way sentences are put together. Most of the time, you will use the correct grammar without even thinking about it. This is because when we learn to speak, read and write, we naturally absorb many of the rules of grammar without realising. However, there are some differences in the way we speak and the way we should write: these differences can lead to grammatical mistakes. Understanding some of the more common grammatical errors will help you in your GCSE exam.

Why is grammar important?

* Using the correct grammar makes your writing clearer.

* Using incorrect grammar makes a bad impression on your reader.

* Understanding grammar will give you the language to talk about your writing.

* Understanding grammar can help you learn other languages.

* Grammatical mistakes will lose you marks in some of your GCSE exams.

Written English has some grammatical rules that will help you avoid common mistakes. For example, a sentence always contains a verb. A sentence without a verb is incomplete and is not suitable for a formal, written exam.

Grammar is not just about accuracy. Improving your understanding of grammar will allow you to improve the impact of your sentences on the reader. Effective grammar can improve the clarity, style and fluency of a sentence.

"Yes, grammar rules do evolve over time, but making up your own to 'stay ahead of the curve' won't work in this English class!"

Word classes

To have a confident grasp of grammar, it is useful to understand the names of different groups of words. These groups are called **word classes**. The main word classes are:

verbs   adjectives   pronouns

nouns   adverbs

Understanding these word classes will give you the language to understand more complicated grammatical ideas. You may already be confident with these word classes as some of them may be familiar from primary school or Key Stage 3.

It is important to remember that some words may appear in more than one group. It depends on how a word is being used in a sentence. For example, the word **sweet**:

- *She gave him a sweet.*

The word **sweet** is functioning here as a noun.

- *He was a sweet puppy.*

The word **sweet** is functioning here as an adjective.

Verbs

Verbs are often described as 'doing words', for example:

run   play   smile

carry   laugh   travel

However, this definition can be misleading. Verbs are not **only** 'doing' words. For example, the words **has** and **were** are also verbs. Verbs can also be 'having' and 'being' words. For example:

am   can   have

is   will   do

STRETCH IT!

The extra verb **was** in this sentence is an example of an auxiliary verb. Other examples of auxiliary verbs are: **be, do, have**. These verbs give more information about the main verbs. For example, in the sentence above, the verb **was** tells us **when** the student revises (in this case, sometime in the past). These verbs are sometimes called 'helping verbs' because they help make the main verb's meaning clearer.

It is useful to remember that verbs are the heart of a sentence. All sentences need at least one main verb.

It is useful to remember that only verbs can show tense (to indicate time). No other word classes can show tense. For example, *The girl is revising hard* or *The girl was going to revise hard.* In one example, the verbs show that the girl is revising hard at the moment and in the other example, the verbs show that the girl is going to revise hard in the future.

NAIL IT!

Sometimes these groups of words are called **parts of speech**. However, the more common term is **word classes** and it is also the name used by the National Curriculum in the UK.

Using the correct tense

Verbs are the only class of word that tell you **when** something has happened. Verbs often change tense to signal the…

past   present   future

Regular verbs follow a set pattern to show **when** something has happened.

Regular verbs	
Present tense	**Past tense**
She walks	She walk**ed**
I love	I lov**ed**
He talks	He talk**ed**
I look	I look**ed**
She wants	She want**ed**

To change these regular verbs to the past tense, you just add the suffix 'ed'.

However, there are also many **irregular verbs** in English.
When these verbs change to the past tense, the root word changes.
For example:

SNAP IT!

Irregular verbs	
Present tense	**Past tense**
They run	They **ran**
I think	**I thought**
I choose	**I chose**
She builds	She **built**
I begin	**I began**
He feels	**He felt**
They drink	They **drank**
She is	She **was**
They do	They **did**

NAIL IT!

Choosing a verb precisely will help the clarity and fluency of your writing. For example:

1 Geothermal energy **can be generated** in areas where magma **lies** close to the surface.
2 Geothermal energy **can be made** in areas where magma **is** close to the surface.
3 Geothermal energy **can be got** in areas where magma **is** close to the surface.

DO IT!

Look carefully at the choice of verbs in bold in the examples in the Nail it! above. Which of these sentences are more effective?

Most English speakers will naturally know which verb form to use, but you may need to revise some of the more challenging irregular verbs.

NAILIT!

History essays are usually written in the past tense, whereas English essays are mostly written in the present tense. Whatever tense you use, it is important to stay in the **same tense** throughout your answer. (See pages 50 and 51 for more details.)

DOIT!

Collect together different essays you have written from a range of subjects (for example, English literature, religious studies, geography or history). Can you spot any verb tense mistakes in your writing? Is there a particular irregular verb that you find difficult? Make a list of your common mistakes and revise the correct verb forms.

Nouns

You may remember that nouns are words that refer to *things*. For example:

| table | book | desk |
| calculator | pen | notes |

However, nouns can also be words that represent *people*, *places* and *ideas*, such as:

| love | teacher | anger |
| Birmingham | journey | Poland |

Nouns can also be divided into proper, common and abstract. Proper nouns are names of people, places and organisations. **Proper nouns should always have a capital letter to signal that they are a name.** Common nouns are all the other nouns that don't belong to the proper noun group. These words do not need a capital letter. An abstract noun is something that cannot be related to the physical senses, so for example, an idea or a feeling.

Proper nouns	Common nouns	Abstract nouns
George	hamster	friendship
Kiran	door	democracy
London	city	anger
Pakistan	country	understanding
Oxfam	child	dream
Save the Children	snow	talent
Scottish Book Trust	horse	poverty
December		childhood
Friday		

SUPPORTIT!

A **determiner** is a word that comes before the noun, to limit the meaning of the noun. For example, the words **a**, **an**, **the** and **every** are determiners. It is not just any car, but **the** car.

Subject and object

The **subject** is the topic of a sentence. Nouns are usually the subject in a sentence. The subject is **who** or **what** does the verb.

A sentence needs at least a subject and a verb to be complete:

Subject	Verb
The woman	shouted

The subject in a sentence can be more than one thing. For example, *The teacher and the student* are arriving. In this sentence the subject is the teacher **and** the student.

The subject can be singular or plural, for example:

- *The teacher* is arriving. (singular)

- *The teachers* are arriving. (plural)

More complicated sentences may have more than one subject and more than one verb. For example:

- *The theatre was* very popular in Elizabethan times, with *all classes* of people *visiting* the theatres.

This sentence has two subjects (The theatre…all classes) and two verbs (was…visiting).

Many sentences also contain an **object**. The object in a sentence is what is acted upon by the subject. The object in a sentence is usually a noun.

The object is usually after the verb in a sentence. Most sentences in the English language follow this grammatical order. For example:

Subject	Verb	Object
The student	sat	the exam.
All classes of people	visited	the theatre.

Verb–subject agreement

In a sentence, it is important that the **subject** agrees with the **verb**. (Remember that the subject is the person or thing doing the verb.) The subject can be singular or plural:

- *The politician is corrupt.* (singular)

- *The politicians are corrupt.* (plural)

If the subject is plural, then the verb must be plural as well. For example:

- *The students is getting organised.* ✗

- *The students are getting organised.* ✔

In the second sentence, the plural subject **students** agrees with the plural verb **are.** If this sentence were singular, using the word **student** rather than **students**, then the verb **is** would be correct:

- *The student is getting organised.*

The subject usually comes before the verb in a sentence.

Underline the subject and highlight the verb in these sentences:

1 London is very busy.
2 The Year 11 students are revising.
3 Sam rides his bike.
4 My sister helps her friends.
5 George and Sam walk to school.

It is useful to remember that **collective nouns** (like staff, flock or class) are counted as a **singular subject** and therefore take a **singular verb**. For example:

- *A protest group was gathering outside the Houses of Parliament.*
- *The choir is ready to rehearse.*

The words **each**, **either** and **neither** are also **singular subjects** and need a **singular verb**.

- *Neither of you is going to the party tonight.*
- *Either history or geography seems a good place to start revision.*

Sometimes, it is difficult to identify the subject if there is a lot of information between the subject and the verb.

- *The play 'Macbeth', one of the most famous plays ever written, is often considered to be Shakespeare's greatest achievement.* ✔
- *The play 'Macbeth', one of the most famous plays ever written, are often considered to be Shakespeare's greatest achievement.* ✗

The first verb form is correct because the subject (the play 'Macbeth') is singular.

- *The play 'Macbeth' and the other major tragedies are often considered to be Shakespeare's greatest achievement.* ✔

This subject–verb agreement is correct here because the subject of the sentence (the play 'Macbeth' and the other major tragedies) is plural.

CONTEXTUALISEIT!

The following religious studies exam answer contains several subject–verb agreement mistakes. As a result, the clarity of the answer is affected and the student would lose marks for their SPaG assessment.

> On Palm Sunday, Jesus ride into Jerusalem humbly on a donkey and the people lie down palm leaves in celebration. Jesus spend 3 days teaching and healing in Jerusalem. On Maundy Thursday, Christians remembers the Last Supper where Jesus celebrates the Passover meal with his disciples. During the meal, Jesus predicts the events that would immediately follow, including his betrayal by Judas, the denial of Peter, his death and resurrection. Jesus shares bread and wine with his Apostles. Good Friday commemorated the crucifixion of Jesus. Easter Saturday is a time for quiet thought and prayer before big celebrations on Easter Sunday.

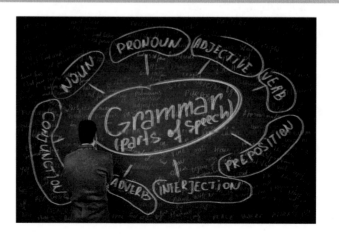

Pronouns

The most commonly used pronouns are pronouns such as **it**, **she**, **he** and **they**. Pronouns can refer to people or things.

Pronouns for people		Pronouns for things
I	me	it
you	she	they
he	him	them
her	us	
we	they	
them		

You can use a pronoun to replace a noun in a sentence, for example:

- *Sarah went to the cinema; Sarah decided to buy some sweets.*
- *Sarah went to the cinema; she decided to buy some sweets.*
- *The exam was difficult; the exam covered topics Ben had not revised.*
- *The exam was difficult; it covered topics Ben had not revised.*

The use of pronouns in the second sentence means that the noun does not have to be repeated.

Unclear pronouns

An unclear use of a pronoun can confuse your reader.

Here is an example taken from an English literature exam:

- *The Gentlewoman tells the Doctor that she has been sleepwalking.* ✗
- *The Gentlewoman tells the Doctor that Lady Macbeth has been sleepwalking.* ✔

The use of the pronoun *she* in the first sentence makes it sound as if the Gentlewoman has been sleepwalking. If the Doctor were female, it could also suggest the Gentlewoman has seen the Doctor sleepwalking. The second sentence replaces the *she* with *Lady Macbeth* to make the meaning of the sentence clear.

The more subjects you put in a sentence and the further away you place them from their matching pronoun, the more likely you are to create confusion. For example:

- *He had a friend and a neighbour who revised with him; he was very good at giving advice.*

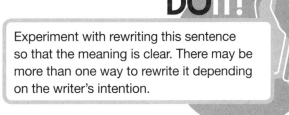

DOIT!

Experiment with rewriting this sentence so that the meaning is clear. There may be more than one way to rewrite it depending on the writer's intention.

CONTEXTUALISEIT!

Avoid using too many pronouns, as they may confuse your reader.

> His propaganda campaign was very powerful: focusing on their economic and social problems and brought widespread support for them. It targeted them by using slogans and policies to win their support. They also made some groups in society scapegoats, which gave them someone to blame.

The history exam answer above uses too many pronouns and is confusing. The meaning of the answer is unclear and marks would be lost for SPaG. The following answer uses fewer pronouns and has more *effective control of meaning*.

> Goebbels' propaganda campaign was very powerful: focusing on the German people's economic and social problems brought widespread support for the Nazi party. The propaganda targeted individual groups by using slogans and policies to win their support. The Nazi party also made some groups in society scapegoats, which gave the German people someone to blame for their problems.

Adjectives

Adjectives are sometimes called 'describing words' because they give more information about the noun or pronoun. Adjectives **do not** give more information about the verb or other adjectives. For example:

- *At the start of the play, Macbeth is presented as a heroic character.*
- *Mount Aso is an active volcano.*
- *Traditional diva lamps are clay pots filled with ghee or oil, with a cotton wick inside.*

Working out if a word is an adjective depends on the position of the word in a sentence.

- *I revised my last topic today.*

In this sentence the word **last** is an adjective because it is giving more information about the noun **topic**.

- *That highlighter didn't last long.*

In this sentence the word **last** is acting as a verb.

Adjectives can appear **before** or **after** the noun in a sentence. For example:

- *The student was tired but opened his books.*
- *The tired student opened his books.*

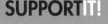

SUPPORTIT!

Avoid using very informal adjectives like *huge* and *massive* in your exam answers.

NAILIT!

Don't overuse adjectives in your exam. In formal writing, one well-chosen adjective is more effective than a string of weak adjectives.

- *Pollution is a huge, bad problem for the environment.* ✗
- *Pollution is a serious problem for the environment.* ✔

Adverbs

Adverbs give more information about the verb, an adjective or another adverb. Adverbs often end in 'ly', but it is important to remember that **not all** adverbs follow this pattern.

For example:

* *She revised **quickly**.*

This adverb gives us more information about the verb **revised**.

* *She did some **very** quick revision.*

This adverb gives use more information about the adjective **quick.**

* *She revised **too** quickly.*

This adverb gives us more information about the adverb **quickly**.

Adverbs can give different types of information, for example:

SNAP IT!

Direction	Frequency	Manner	Time	Place
She walked *ahead/away/ back*.	She *always/ rarely/often* walked to work.	She walked *slowly/quickly/ angrily*.	She will walk to work *today/ now/tomorrow*.	She walked *outside/ downstairs/here*.

A word's class can change depending on how it is used in a sentence.

* *She made notes faster than her friend.*

The word **faster** is adding more information to the verb **made**, so the word is functioning as an adverb.

* *She is faster at making notes than her friend.*

In this sentence, the word **faster** is adding more information to the pronoun **she**, so the word is functioning as an adjective.

Conjunctions and linking words

Conjunctions are the linking words in a sentence. For example:

* *I took regular breaks, so I could stay focused.*
* *I revised English and made some notes.*
* *I revised English, then had a break.*

Your writing will often benefit from using a variety of linking words, rather than relying just on the words **and** and **then**.

Some adverbs can also be used at the start of a sentence to make a link to the previous sentence. For example:

* *Eric is presented as a spoilt young man. However, later in the play we see that he is one of the few characters to show genuine remorse for his actions.*

Linking words can be divided into the following useful groups:

SNAPIT!

Sequencing	Comparing	Qualifying
next	equally	however
then	similarly	although
meanwhile	likewise	despite
after	in comparison	except
finally		unless
Contrasting	**Cause and effect**	**Emphasising**
whereas	consequently	especially
in contrast	so	notably
alternatively	therefore	significantly
otherwise	because	

Sentence structure

You can often improve the clarity, style and fluency of your sentences by:

- *varying the type of sentence used*
- *varying how the sentence starts*
- *varying sentence length.*

There are three types of sentence: simple, complex and compound.

SNAPIT!

Type of sentence	Definition	Example
Simple sentence	A sentence that has one main verb.	She **ran** very fast down the road.
Compound sentence	A sentence that has more than one verb. The two parts of the sentence are equal.	She **ran** very fast down the road, but she **was** late for her exam. She **ran** very fast down the road; she **was** late for her exam.
Complex sentence	A sentence that has more than one verb. It also usually links a simple sentence to a clause that doesn't make sense on its own.	*Although she **was** very tired,* she **ran** very fast down the road.

Here is another example of how variety in sentence structure can improve clarity:

- *It is important to remember that Eva Smith is a symbol of all working class women and this symbolism is reinforced by her common surname.*

Can be changed to:

- *Importantly, Eva Smith can be seen as a symbol of all working class women. Her common surname reinforces this symbolism.*

Experiment with the following sentences. Rewrite the sentences, changing the word order, the length and type of sentence (for example, change a simple to a complex sentence). What are the effects of these changes? Do any of the changes improve clarity, style or fluency of the sentences?

> Some religions have special ceremonies. Like when a child is born. Just after the birth of a baby, in some Hindu families, the family get some honey and write the sacred syllable aum on the baby's tongue. Monks may be invited into the home, in some Buddhist homes, after the birth of a baby. The monks prepare a horoscope. The horoscope will then decide the name.

Using Standard English

Standard English is the 'correct' way to speak or write in formal situations. It is the version of the English language that is accepted and used by the government, the law courts and the media. BBC newsreaders use Standard English when they deliver the news.

 STRETCH IT!

> The idea of Standard English is fairly modern in historical terms. A wide range of different versions of English have always been spoken across the country. The idea of a 'correct' or 'standard' version only started to develop when the printing press became widely used in the 15th century.

Spoken and written language

It is useful to know that the way you speak is not necessarily the way you should write. Most people don't use Standard English all the time when they are speaking.

When we speak, we naturally break some of the rules of Standard English grammar. However, in a formal situation (like a job interview or written exam answer) it is important to use Standard English. For example:

- *I <u>have been</u> studying social care for three years.*

- *I <u>should have</u> studied harder for that exam.*

- *<u>I am going to</u> study hard.*

NAIL IT!

It is a very common mistake to write **should of** or **could of** in exams instead of **should have** and **could have**. This is probably because **should've** and **could've** in spoken language sound like **should of** and **could of**.

The word **gonna** is an informal contraction that means **going to**. It is commonly used in spoken language. However, because it is an example of non-standard English, it should never be used in an exam.

Many English speakers use the word **ain't** in their everyday spoken language, for example, *If it ain't broke, don't fix it.*

The informal contraction aint is used in a wide range of spoken contexts. For example, it can mean:

am not	is not	have not
are not	has not	was not

However, this feature of spoken language is **not** suitable for written language and is not part of Standard English grammar. Using the contraction **ain't** in a written exam will lose you marks for your SPaG assessment.

Double negatives

Using a double negative is common in some forms of spoken English. For example, *I have never done nothing like that.*

However, double negatives are not part of Standard English and should **never** be used in written English.

In Standard English the following sentence would be used instead: I have done nothing like that **or** I have never done anything like that.

Rewrite this sentence so that it uses Standard English.

Working class people **didn't** have **no** voting rights in the early 19th century.

NAIL IT!

Using double negatives in your exam will lose you marks for your SPaG assessment. If you have used the word **no** in a double negative sentence, try replacing the word **no** with **any**.

How to use paragraphs

Paragraphs divide up your writing into chunks so that it is easier to read. Paragraphs also signal to the reader that you are starting a new point or subject within your writing. You can either leave a whole line between paragraphs or indent the first line. Both ways are acceptable in a written exam, but you must stick to the same method. Don't swap half way through your essay.

The purpose of a paragraph is to give your writing a clear overall structure. For example, if you are developing an argument your paragraphs will signal shifts and stages in that argument.

It is important that you use clearly marked paragraphs in your shorter answers and longer essays.

There is no set rule about how long a paragraph should be. However, as a rough guide, paragraphs should be no shorter than two or three sentences. Most paragraphs in an essay will average about four to six sentences.

 SUPPORTIT!

If you realise that you have forgotten to add paragraphs in your exam, you can add the symbol // to show where the breaks should be. However, don't rely upon this method. You will get more marks if you signpost the paragraphs correctly when you write your answer initially.

 **CHECK**IT!

1 Using your knowledge from this section, write at least a paragraph arguing against the following statement:

A knowledge of grammar is not important in the 21st century.

2 Which class of word should be at the heart of a sentence?

3 Experiment with the following paragraph, changing the grammar to add clarity and fluency to the sentences. You could consider:

- changing the length of the sentences
- varying the way the sentences start
- changing the type of sentence (for example, from simple to complex sentences)
- adding or changing conjunctions
- removing unnecessary adverbs or adjectives.

Theatre was really very popular during Shakespeare's lifetime. People from all different sorts of classes would make up the audience. Women did not act on stage. Acting was not seen as an appropriate, nice employment for women. The female roles were often played by young, adolescent boys. The Elizabethan ideas of gender were really very different from our ideas in the 21st century. Young boys were seen as having feminine qualities. Then the young boys could dress up more convincingly as women. In the Elizabethan times the term boy didn't refer to children. The term 'boy' could refer to anyone who has not entered puberty. Lady Macbeth was probably played by a young boy and older actors would play older female roles.

4 What should be used instead of **should of** and **could of** in a written exam?

5 Why should the word **ain't** be avoided in a written exam?

Grammar: English literature

Introduction and advice

In your English literature exam, you are aiming to write a clear and well-developed essay. Using accurate grammar is important as it will enable you to make your meaning clear to the reader. You don't want the examiner to puzzle over your sentences in order to work out your meaning. Effective use of grammar will also give you more control over your analysis of texts and allow you to develop more complex and subtle ideas.

Conjunctions and linking words

In an English literature exam, conjunctions and other linking words can give your writing more control. They can help guide your argument and encourage you to move beyond a description of the text.

CONTEXTUALISEIT!

The following exam answer extract uses conjunctions and other linking words with *consistent accuracy* in order give *effective control of meaning*. This answer would therefore be assessed as meeting the high performance criteria for the SPaG assessment.

> Mrs Birling insists that the man involved should take responsibility for what happened to Eva Smith, whereas the audience realises the irony of this statement because they suspect that Eric is responsible. Eric's absence from the stage at this point in the play is essential for building the tension. Despite Sheila also realising that Eric is involved, Mrs Birling only slowly becomes aware of her son's involvement. Sheila tries to make her mother understand, '...but don't you see...' and then later '...now, Mother don't you see?'. Significantly, Mrs Birling does not fully understand until the end of Act Two, so the action ends on a dramatic moment.

NAILIT!

Don't overuse connectives in your English literature essay. Starting **every** sentence with a connective can make your writing sound unnatural.

Tense

English literature essays are usually written in the present tense. For example:

- *Mr Birling <u>gives</u> a speech to his family about the Titanic being unsinkable. This speech <u>shows</u> the audience that Mr. Birling is not to be trusted.*

Make sure you stay in the same tense. For example, the following answer changes tense in the second sentence.

- Mr Birling <u>gives</u> a speech to his family about the Titanic being unsinkable. This speech <u>showed</u> the audience that Mr Birling is not to be trusted.

The only exception to this rule is when you are writing about the life of the author, poet or playwright. In this instance it is fine to use the **past tense**:

- *Charles Dickens <u>was</u> a social critic as well as a writer of fiction.*

DOIT!

Rewrite the following sentences, so that the correct tense is used.

1 In Shakespeare's time, many people believe in the supernatural.
2 In his play, Willy Russell showed the difference between social classes.
3 Ralph and Piggy were shown as the more moral characters in the novel.
4 At the beginning of the novel, Austen described the difference between the sisters.
5 The author, Sir Arthur Conan Doyle, is a trained doctor.

Paragraphs

Your English literature exam may require you to write long essays. Paragraphs are very important in long essays, as they help the examiner follow your ideas.

It is helpful to start each paragraph with a topic sentence. A topic sentence clearly introduces your main point and signals to the reader what the paragraph will be about. For example:

The poet uses structure to emphasise the unchanging nature of life in the trenches. *The first four lines of each stanza has the rhyming pattern of abba. This regularity mirrors the routine of daily life as nothing is changing in the rhyme scheme and nothing is changing for the soldiers. The repetition of the line 'But nothing happens,' intensifies this effect and leaves the reader with a sense of the soldier's frustration and boredom.*

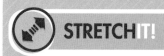

STRETCH IT!

To make your essay structure more sophisticated, make sure each paragraph links to the focus of the exam question.

SUPPORT IT!

Writing a quick plan will help you organise your ideas into clear paragraphs. The points in your plan could become your topic sentences.

Grammar: Geography

Nouns

Nouns are words that refer to *people*, *places* and *objects* (and sometimes *events*).

Proper nouns

It is important to remember when nouns are proper nouns as they need capital letters.

Pronouns

In geography, try not to use personal pronouns such as 'I', 'me' and 'you'. It is preferable to use words such as 'they', 'them', 'that' and 'which'. This is because readers may regard comments in the first person as being subjective.

Verb–subject agreement

Verbs are also known as *doing*, *being* or *having* words.

It is important that the subject and verb in your sentences agree. In this example, the subject is 'farmer' and the verb is 'grow':

- *The subsistence <u>farmer</u> <u>grows</u> crops to support her family.*

Or if there were more than one farmer (plural):

- *The subsistence <u>farmers</u> <u>grow</u> crops to support their families.*

Conjunctions

Using conjunctions (joining words) in geography can make all the difference to the quality of your answer. They help you to put your responses into context, to provide more detail and to show the connection between points.

Rewrite each of the following sentences using the best conjunction from this list: or, but, although, so, and, unless.

1 The birth rate in Japan is very low. There is an ageing population.
2 Urbanisation occurs rapidly in LIDCs. Slums develop on the outskirts of cities.
3 Development requires social, economic and environmental consideration. Sustainability will not be achieved.
4 Tectonic activity happens at plate margins. Hotspot volcanoes occur in the middle of plates.
5 Earthquake prediction is still almost impossible. Earthquake preparation in risk areas can save lives.
6 Long-term development aid is more sustainable. There is an emergency, such as a natural disaster.

Paragraphs

Using paragraphs effectively will enable you to structure long written answers well. Planning is critical to good structure.

The 'BUG' technique is an effective way to understand a question in order to structure a good answer. BUG stands for: **Box** the command word, **Underline** the key words, **Go** back and check again.

Evaluate the <u>effectiveness</u> of the <u>response</u> to a <u>hazard</u> you have studied.

The command word is 'evaluate' so the examiner will be looking for the ways in which the response was and was not effective. Following this 'BUG' principle you can prepare to write the following paragraphs:

1 An introduction of the hazard chosen with background information.
2 Examples showing when the response was positive.
3 Examples showing when the response was negative.
4 A conclusion including the word 'effective'.

For each paragraph you can use the PEEL technique (Point, Evidence, Explanation, Link). In other words:

- (P) Make your **point**.
- (E) Provide **evidence** to justify it.
- (E) **Explain** the significance.
- (L) **Link** it to the question.

BUG and PEEL to structure great answers.

B – Box the command word
U – Underline the key word
G – Go back and check

P – Point
E – Evidence
E – Explain
L – Link

Grammar: History

PEEL paragraphs

To achieve the highest marks available for SPaG you must have *effective control of meaning in the context demands of the question*. This means that you need to be focused on the question and structure your answer well to make sure that your meaning is clear. In order to help with your structure and layout in the longer answers for GCSE history, it is important to have focused paragraphs. The SPaG marks will usually come in the questions with the highest marks and therefore the examiner will expect a longer piece of writing that is focused and includes historical detail.

PEEL stands for Point, Evidence, Explain, Link. This gives you a framework for each of your paragraphs.

- Point = what you are going to be discussing in the paragraph.
- Evidence = historical facts and detail that supports the point.
- Explain = why the facts agree or disagree with the point.
- Link = back to the question making a judgement on the question as a whole.

NAIL IT!

It may help you to write PEEL down the margin of the page when you are practising the longer answers to remind you when you start each paragraph and whether it is clear.

CONTEXTUALISE IT!

How significant was warfare between 1640 and 1660 for British society?

> Warfare made a very significant impact on British society between 1640 and 1660. During this time Britain experienced a Civil War which led to huge numbers of men being involved in the fighting. Sometimes families were split because people picked a side. Around 200,000 people were killed during the Civil War, including women who followed the battles and were often involved in nursing the soldiers. This shows that the war was significant as so many people were involved. Britain's population at the time was small so the proportion who were killed would have had a huge impact on society. This makes the time between 1640 and 1660 very significant for British society as the war affected so many.

Focused start making clear use of the question

Interesting point but needs to have evidence to back this up

Clear judgement here linking to the question

Making judgements

Most exam boards have an explicit question asking you to make a judgement, usually phrased as, *How far do you agree...* It is important in this case to be decisive and to make a clear judgement, supported with evidence. You may agree or disagree with the question, as long as you support whatever point you are trying to make with evidence.

STRETCH IT!

In order to achieve the highest marks and make your point even more effective, you can make a measured judgement. That means rather than saying, *I agree because...* you can say, *I strongly agree because...* or, *I partly agree because...* This makes it convincing that you have considered your argument.

DO IT!

Read the questions below and write a clear opening judgement on the topic. If you can, make it a measured judgement.

1 How far do you agree that Chinese society suffered during the Cultural Revolution?
2 How far do you agree that the main reason Hitler came to power was due to the Great Depression?
3 How far do you agree that the Tsar was the main reason for the October Revolution in 1917?
4 How far do you agree that the Civil Rights Act came about due to the assassination of John F Kennedy?
5 How far do you agree that Anglo-Saxon society was completely changed by the invasion of William, Duke of Normandy?

Grammar: Religious studies

Appropriate writing style

In your exam answers you need to use formal language and avoid slang. You need to sound as professional as possible. Imagine you are practising communicating with a future boss or client: you need to be on your best linguistic behaviour. Many employers are looking for staff who can write well technically and also have an understanding of how language affects the audience. When you are practising at home you can use a dictionary or thesaurus to embellish your language.

Power up your language!

Set yourself apart from other candidates by using sophisticated language. However, make sure you know what the words and phrases mean! Try to include some of the following phrases in your longer answers.

DO IT!

Write down more formal versions of these responses (you could try finishing the sentences with relevant exam style answers):

1 Yes but…
2 Many people think it is ok…
3 No because…
4 I kind of agree with this…
5 This is rubbish because…

SNAP IT!

Explaining	Comparing	Applying knowledge	Justifying an opinion	Analysing	Evaluating
This means…	Similarly…	The main source for this belief is…	I think… because…	If we accept this then…	The most convincing argument is…
To illustrate…	Likewise…	As a result of this…	I agree with this because…	However, this conflicts with the teaching on… which says…	This is a weak argument because…
In particular…	On the other hand…	One teaching which supports this is…	The main reason I think this is because…	The key idea is…	A particular strength of this is…
For example…	Alternatively…	Many Christians would argue… because…	This is logical because…	This follows the theme of…	The strongest argument in favour of this is…
Notably…	This is similar to…because…	Some Buddhists would argue… because…			
In addition to this…	In the same way…				
In spite of this…					

Analysis and evaluation

Whichever exam board you are following, there are two common Assessment Objectives (AOs) in religious studies.

- AO1: Demonstrate knowledge and understanding of religion and beliefs including:

  - beliefs, practices and sources of authority

  - influence on individuals, communities and societies

  - similarities and differences within and/or between religions and beliefs.

- AO2: Analyse and evaluate aspects of religion and belief, including their significance and influence.

The SPaG marks and Quality of Writing marks are always allocated in the longest, AO2 questions so you need to practise analysing and evaluating the statements that you are given.

Clear analysis is comparing and contrasting ideas (saying how they are similar or different) as well as organising your ideas clearly with an introduction and a logical line of argument from paragraph to paragraph. It can also mean explaining an idea in more detail.

You could try some of these sentence starters:

- *This shows that...*
- *This means...*
- *This reveals...*
- *This expresses the idea that...*

- *This implies...*
- *This suggests...*
- *This confirms...*
- *This highlights the difference between...*

Evaluation comes from considering more than one side of an argument and then concluding which argument is best, with clear reasons **why** you think it is the best. To add more arguments, try starting each paragraph with one of these phrases:

- *Also, ...*
- *Another essential point is...*
- *Additionally, ...*

- *Equally, ...*
- *Furthermore, ...*
- *In addition, ...*
- *Likewise, ...*

- *Secondly, ...*
- *Similarly, ...*
- *Subsequently, ...*
- *Moreover, ...*

You then want to offer an alternative view. You could use these sentence starters:

- *However, ...*
- *Alternatively, ...*
- *This is in contrast to ...*

- *On the other hand, ...*
- *In comparison, ...*

You want to have more arguments on the side you agree with, or stronger arguments on the side you agree with so you can reach a clear conclusion using one of these phrases:

- *In summary, ...*
- *In conclusion, ...*
- *Thus, ...*

- *It seems clear that...*
- *Overall,...*

DO IT!

'A married couple is the best family unit in which to raise children.' Evaluate this statement giving reasons and showing that you have thought about more than one point of view. You must refer to religious teachings in your answer.

Exam tips

Before the exam

- Make a list of all your GCSE exams and then divide each of these into topics. (You can download the **free** revision app to help you!)
- These topic lists should form the content for your revision.
- Create a revision timetable, making sure you cover all your topics.
- Aim to cover each topic at least three times during your revision period.
- Start revising around eight weeks before your first exam.
- Don't just read through your notes. Try rewriting your notes in a different format, for example, a mind map or a diagram.
- Don't just revise using a tablet or computer: handwrite some of your revision. Handwriting words can also help your long-term memory.
- Find a quiet place to revise without distractions.
- Take regular breaks during your revision.
- Make time to exercise. Research has shown that regular exercise helps your brain to stay alert.
- The night before your exam, try not to do lots of last-minute revision. Instead, try to get an early night.

On the day of the exam

- Give yourself plenty of time to get ready.
- Eat a healthy breakfast.
- Check your exam timetable again: what time do you have to be there? Which room is the exam in?
- Check if you need any special equipment for the exam.
- Check you have your centre number and candidate number.

During the exam

- Read the exam paper carefully and double check you have selected the right questions.
- Be aware of the time and make rough estimates of how long to spend on each section of the exam.
- If you have any extra time at the end of the exam, carefully proofread your answers for mistakes.
- If you spot a mistake, carefully write the correction above and put a line through the mistake.
- If you need to use a tricky specialist word, check to see if the spelling is given on the question paper.

Glossary

abbreviation   A shortened version of a word (for example, **eg** comes from the Latin 'exempli gratia' and means '**for example**').

adjective   A word that gives more information about the noun or pronoun (the **tired** student).

adverb   A word that gives more information about the verb, an adjective or another adverb (**very**, **quickly**, **here**, **often**).

apostrophe   A punctuation mark (**'**) used to show either possession (Sally's pen) or missing letters (can't).

brackets   Punctuation marks (** **) used to contain part of a sentence.

colon   A punctuation mark (**:**) used before a list of items, a quotation, an expansion or an explanation.

comma   A punctuation mark (**,**) that shows a pause between parts of a sentence or separates items in a list.

conjunction   The linking words in a sentence. They can be used within a sentence or at the start of a sentence to link to the idea in the previous sentence (**and**, **then**, **however**).

consonant   A letter in the alphabet that is not a vowel.

contraction   When two or more words are shortened by removing letters (for example, **would have** becomes **would've**).

dash   A punctuation mark (**–**) that can replace a comma, colon or bracket, or show a relationship between numbers (for example, 15-20).

determiner   A word that determines the noun (such as **a**, **an** and **the**).

ellipsis   A punctuation mark (**...**) to show that something is missing from a sentence.

etymology   The origin and meaning of words and how they have changed through history

exclamation mark   A punctuation mark (**!**) used to show strong emotion or surprise.

full stop   A punctuation mark (**.**) used to show that a sentence has ended.

homophone   A word that sounds the same as another, but has a different spelling and meaning (**their** and **there**).

hyphen   A punctuation mark (**-**) used to join words or sections of words together.

inverted commas   Another term for quotation or speech marks.

noun   A word that represents an object, people, place or idea (**love**, **town**, **table**, **London**).

object   The object in a sentence is acted upon by the subject. The object is usually a noun. For example: The girl swam in the **river**.

plural   More than one of something (**students**, **babies**).

prefix   A letter or group of letters added to the beginning of a word (**anti**dote, **auto**matic).

pronoun   A word used instead of a noun in a sentence (**she**, **he**, **their**, **everyone**).

question mark   A punctuation mark **(?)** used at the end of a question.

quotation   A piece of text taken from a longer text.

quotation marks   A pair of punctuation marks (**double** "" **or single** ') used around a quotation.

semicolon   A punctuation mark **(;)** used to connect two sentences.

singular   One of something (**student**, **baby**).

subject   The subject is who or what is doing the verb. Nouns are usually the subject in a sentence. For example, **She** walked.

suffix   A letter or group of letters added to the end of a word (imagina**tion**, happ**ily**).

tense   The tense of a verb tells us when something happens (**the past**, **present** or **future**).

verb   A 'doing', 'being' or 'having' word (**running**, **cried**, **is**, **are**).

vowel   The letters **a**, **e**, **i**, **o**, **u**.

Answers

SPELLING

Page 8

Do it!

Answers will be personal responses.

Page 9

Do it!

1 know
2 climb
3 before
4 knock
5 playwright
6 Bible

Page 14

Do it!

different, across, quietly, regretful, until, accident, accommodation, attempt, finally, harassed, called, suffering, embarrassment

Page 15

Do it!

Answers will be personal responses.

Page 16

Do it!

Answers will be personal responses.

Page 17

Do it!

Answers could include: American spelling often removes a silent letter so that the spelling of the word matches the sound (for example, removing the 'u' from colour, labour and neighbour). American uses 'er' instead of 're' at the end of words and 'ze' endings rather than 'se' endings.

Page 18

Do it! (middle)

Answers could include:

1 The girl had a break from her revision. / The brake on the car had failed.
2 The boy walked through the tunnel. / The boy threw the ball.
3 The man asked the people whether they had seen his dog. / The weather was too poor for the men to climb the mountain.
4 The woman passed her driving test. / The ball flew past the car.

Do it! (bottom)

Answers will be personal responses.

Page 19

Do it!

I'm grateful to live in a peaceful country where we don't have to worry about violence on the streets. There are lots of reasons to feel safe. In the past there were wars in this country, but now there is not so much unrest in the UK. We know that we are lucky to go to school and if we lose our job there are people to help.

Check it!

1 Homophones and names.
2 *Answers will vary, but may refer to:*
   - usually: double letters, suffix rules
   - valuable: removing the 'e' from 'value' and adding suffix
   - occasion: double letters, 'sion' not 'tion'
   - together: not two words
   - centre: watch for American spelling – center
   - February: silent letter 'r'
   - especially: double letters, suffix rules
3 consistent accuracy

ENGLISH LITERATURE

Page 20

Do it!

Answers will be personal responses.

GEOGRAPHY

Page 22

Do it!

1 Business
2 Communication
   Desert
4 Environment
5 Global
6 Government
7 Precipitation
8 Seismic
9 Sustainable
10 Temperature

Page 23

Do it! (top)

1 Volcanoes
2 Businesses
3 Economies
4 Countries
5 Cities
6 Counties
7 Valleys
8 Reefs

Do it! (bottom)

The <u>Boscastle floods devastated</u> a small Cornish fishing <u>village</u> in 2004. After an unprecedented amount of <u>precipitation</u> fell, the water level <u>rose</u> quickly because the village lay at the <u>confluence</u> of the <u>two</u> rivers: Jordan and <u>Valency</u>. The rescue efforts <u>were</u> excellent: <u>seven</u> helicopters were <u>brought</u> in <u>to</u> rescue people off roofs. Because of the quick response by the emergency services, the <u>death toll</u> was zero and the injury <u>toll</u> was one. A man broke his thumb.

HISTORY

Page 24

Do it!

Answers will be personal responses.

Page 25

Do it! (top)

Answers will be personal responses.

Do it! (bottom)

1 The <u>government</u> had a policy of <u>centralisation</u>.
2 The <u>reign</u> of Henry VIII was marked by <u>foreign</u> wars and <u>political</u> problems.
3 <u>Soldiers</u> were using <u>weapons</u> that were provided by the United States.
4 A system of <u>hierarchy</u> existed in the country during the <u>medieval</u> times.

RELIGIOUS STUDIES

Page 26

Do it!

Answers will be personal responses.

Page 27

Do it!

1 Revel<u>ation</u>
2 Crucifix<u>ion</u>
3 Ascen<u>sion</u>
4 Denomin<u>ation</u>
5 Confe<u>ssion</u>
6 Medit<u>ation</u>

Do it! (centre)

Answers will be personal responses.

Do it! (bottom)

Answers will be personal responses.

PUNCTUATION

Page 28

Do it!

Answers will be personal responses.

Page 30

Do it!

Bob Cratchit is presented to the reader in a sympathetic way, as we are encouraged to pity the character. Scrooge, by contrast, represents those members of the upper classes who shut themselves off from the rest of the community. In order to feel glad at the end of the story, the readers need to dislike him at the start. Cratchit is a symbol of the moral poor. Scrooge is a symbol of the greedy rich.

Page 33

Do it!

1 ✗
2 ✔
3 ✗

Page 34

Do it!

1 When analysing poetry, it is important to focus on three main areas: language, form and structure.
2 Chalk is a permeable rock: it lets water through.

Page 35

Do it!

1 The First World War (1914–18) drew in all the world's powerful countries.
2 Earthquakes are detected by seismographs (electromagnetic sensors that translate ground motions into electrical changes).
3 In the Jewish religion, the most important day of the week is Shabbat (the Sabbath).

Page 40

Check it!

1 Any two of the following reasons:
- Punctuation adds clarity to your writing.
- When used accurately, punctuation marks give you more control over your meaning and tone.
- A punctuation mark in the wrong place could change the whole meaning of your writing.
- If you use accurate punctuation, you will pick up more marks in some of your exams.
2 Answers may vary. For example:

Mr Birling is an important character: he is the head of the Birling family. He dominates the first part of the play with long speeches; the content of these speeches shows he is out of touch with society. He is presented as a pompous, over confident and selfish character.
3 *Results will vary. Check definitions against the glossary on pages 71 and 72.*
4 b To signal that part of the sentence is missing in a quotation.
5 *Answers will be personal responses.*

ENGLISH LITERATURE

Page 42

Do it!

Answers will be personal responses.

Page 41

Do it!

Double or single quotation marks are acceptable in this answer.

1 In Act 1 of *An Inspector Calls* the character of Mr Birling states that "The Germans don't want war. Nobody wants war…"
2 The playwright focuses on the theme of class in Act 2: the narrator states that "…what we, the English, have come to know as class?"

GEOGRAPHY

Page 43

Do it! (top)

Bristol

the park

Hollywood Boulevard

Mumbai

Kingston upon Thames

New York City

a city

Pacific Ocean

the ocean

The Democratic Republic of Congo

Do it! (bottom)

Example topics where a colon and a list would be useful:

- Amendments you could make around the house to be prepared for an earthquake.
- Flora and fauna within an ecosystem.
- Conditions required for a tropical storm to form.

Page 44

Do it!

1 The government's policies aimed to reduce poverty.
2 Johannesburg's slum areas have high crime rates.

HISTORY

Page 45

Do it!

1 20th century = any date between 1900 and 1999
2 234 = 3rd century
3 14th century = any date between 1300 and 1399
4 1781 = 18th century
5 1398 = 14th century
6 467 = 5th century
7 17th century = any date between 1600 and 1699
8 6th century = any date between 500 and 599
9 1066 = 11th century
10 1555 = 16th century

Page 46

Do it! (top)

1000–1500	Middle Ages, Medieval
1500–1700	Early Modern, Tudor
1700–1900	Industrial Age, Victorian, Georgian
1900–present	Modern Age, 20th century, Technological Age

Do it! (bottom)

Women during World War One worked hard in a range of industries. At the start of the war, the leader of the Suffragettes, Emmeline Pankhurst, along with her daughter Christabel, called for an end to their campaigning in order to support the soldiers fighting in France and Belgium. This led to women working in munitions factories as well as other industries to help support the front line. After the war, the Home Secretary, George Cave, introduced the Representation of the People Act 1918 which, when passed, allowed some women the right to vote. Only in 1928 did women gain equal terms with men.

RELIGIOUS STUDIES

Page 48

Do it! (top)

(Taken from the New International Version)

Genesis 2: 22–24

[22] Then the Lord God made a woman from the rib[a] he had taken out of the man, and he brought her to the man. [23] The man said, "This is now bone of my bones and flesh of my flesh; she shall be called 'woman,' for she was taken out of man." [24] That is why a man leaves his father and mother and is united to his wife, and they become one flesh.

Matthew 19: 4–6

[4] "Haven't you read," he replied, "that at the beginning the Creator 'made them male and female,' [5] and said, 'For this reason a man will leave his father and mother and be united to his wife, and the two will become one flesh'? [6] So they are no longer two, but one flesh. Therefore what God has joined together, let no one separate."

Mark 10: 11–12

[11] He answered, "Anyone who divorces his wife and marries another woman commits adultery against her. [12] And if she divorces her husband and marries another man, she commits adultery."

Exodus 20: 14

[14] "You shall not commit adultery."

1 Corinthians 7: 10–11

[10] To the married I give this command (not I, but the Lord): A wife must not separate from her husband. [11] But if she does, she must remain unmarried or else be reconciled to her husband. And a husband must not divorce his wife.

Do it! (middle)

1 Siddhartha Gautama <u>could have</u> stayed in the palace all his life.

2 Christians <u>should have</u> done more to save the environment.

3 Malala Yusafzai <u>would have</u> still spoken out for girls' rights even if she had not been shot by the Taliban.

GRAMMAR

Page 51

Do it!

'Geothermal energy **can be generated** in areas where magma **lies** close to the surface': this is the most effective sentence, because the verbs are more precise.

Page 52

Do it!

Answers will be personal responses.

Page 53

Do it!

1 <u>London</u> is very busy.

2 <u>The year 11 students</u> are revising.

3 <u>Sam</u> rides his bike.

4 <u>My sister</u> helps her friends.

5 <u>George and Sam</u> walk to school.

Page 54

Contextualise it!

On Palm Sunday, <u>Jesus rode</u> into Jerusalem humbly on a donkey and <u>the people lay</u> down palm leaves in celebration. <u>Jesus spent</u> 3 days teaching and healing in Jerusalem. On Maundy Thursday, <u>Christians remember</u> the Last Supper where <u>Jesus celebrated</u> the Passover meal with his disciples. During the meal, <u>Jesus predicted</u> the events that would immediately follow, including his betrayal by Judas; the denial of Peter, his death and resurrection. <u>Jesus shared</u> bread and wine with his Apostles. Good Friday <u>commemorates</u> the crucifixion of Jesus. Easter Saturday is a time for quiet thought and prayer before big celebrations on Easter Sunday.

Page 55

Do it!

Answers may vary. For example:

He had a friend and a neighbour who revised with him. The friend was very good at giving advice.

He had a friend, who was very good at giving advice, and a neighbour who revised with him.

Page 59

Do it!

Answers will vary. For example:

Some religions have special ceremonies when a child is born. For example, in some Hindu families, just after the birth of a baby, the family write the sacred syllable aum on the baby's tongue with honey. In some Buddhist homes, Monks may be invited into the home after the birth of a baby; they prepare a horoscope that decides the baby's name.

Page 60

Do it!

Working class people didn't have any voting rights in the early 19th century.

Page 61

Check it!

1   *The argument against the statement may contain some of the following points:*
    - Using the correct grammar gives your writing clarity.
    - Using incorrect grammar makes a negative impression on your reader.
    - Understanding grammar will give you the language to talk about your writing.
    - Understanding grammar can help you learn other languages.
    - Grammatical mistakes will lose you marks in some of your GCSE exams.
2   A verb should be at the heart of a sentence.
3   *Answers will vary. For example:*
    During Shakespeare's lifetime, the theatre was very popular, with people from all different classes in the audience. Because acting was not seen as an appropriate employment for women, the female roles were often played by young boys. The Elizabethan ideas of gender were different from our ideas in the 21st century: young boys were seen as having feminine qualities. Therefore, the young boys could dress up more convincingly as women. In the Elizabethan times the term 'boy' refers not to children, but rather to anyone who has not entered puberty. Lady Macbeth was probably played by a young boy, whereas older female characters could be played by older actors.
4   **Should have** and **could have**.
5   The word **ain't** should be avoided because it is an informal contraction and is not part of Standard English grammar.

ENGLISH LITERATURE

Page 63

Do it!

1   In Shakespeare's time, many people <u>believed</u> in the supernatural.
2   In his play, Willy Russell <u>shows</u> the difference between social classes.
3   Ralph and Piggy <u>are</u> shown as the more moral characters in the novel.
4   At the beginning of the novel, Austen <u>describes</u> the difference between the sisters.
5   The author, Sir Arthur Conan Doyle, <u>was</u> a trained doctor.

GEOGRAPHY

Do it! (right)

Answers could include:

2   Climate change: atmosphere, fossil fuels, CO_2, methane, sea level
3   Rivers: meander, ox-bow lake, delta, river cliff, river beach, V-shaped valley
4   Ecosystems: environment, climate, abiotic factors, biotic factors, vegetation
5   Urban growth: migrants, slums, Central Business District, suburbs, inner city
6   Development: aid, trade, investment, poverty, growth
7   Population: migration, birth rate, infant mortality, life expectancy, population structure
8   Migration: people, international migration, push factors, pull factors, remittances

Page 64 (top left)

Do it!

city, London, UN Headquarters, mountain, river, Aberdeen, city centre, Birmingham City Centre, epicentre, Oxfam, slum, Dharavi

Do it (top right)

Answers will vary.

Do it! (bottom)

Answers will vary. For example:

A charity exists to support those in need of help.

When a volcano erupts, hot lava flows from it.

A river changes shape as it flows from its source to its mouth.

Page 65

Do it!

1   The birth rate in Japan is very low **so** there is an ageing population.

2   Urbanisation occurs rapidly in LIDCs **and** slums develop on the outskirts of cities.

3   Development requires social, economic and environmental consideration **or** sustainability will not be achieved.

4   Tectonic activity happens at plate margins **but** hotspot volcanoes occur in the middle of plates.

5   Earthquake prediction is still almost impossible **although** earthquake preparation in risk areas can save lives.

6   Long-term development aid is more sustainable **unless** there is an emergency, such as a natural disaster.

Page 66

Do it! (bottom)

Answers will be personal responses

Do it!

These words could be associated with many different topics but answers could include:

*   explode: tectonic activity
*   migrate: population
*   transport: rivers
*   communicate: development

HISTORY

Page 67

Do it!

1   Chinese society suffered greatly during the Cultural Revolution as collectives were formed between the years 1966-76, which caused problems for the general population.

2   The most important factor in Hitler's rise to power was the Depression in Germany as it led to around 30% of people being unemployed; many turned to Hitler as he promised to end unemployment.

3   I strongly agree that the Tsar was the main reason for the October Revolution as he was a poor military leader. When he went to the front line in 1915, this caused problems as he left his German wife in charge of the country, and Russia was fighting Germany.

4   The assassination of John F Kennedy was of vital importance in bringing about the Civil Rights Act. When Lyndon B Johnson became president, he vowed to push the Civil Rights Bill through to law as a tribute to Kennedy, and the shock of Kennedy's assassination caused many to support the bill.

5   Anglo-Saxon society was hugely changed by the invasion of William I: the invasion led to new castles being built all over the country and the old Saxon earls were removed and replaced with Norman knights and lords.

RELIGIOUS STUDIES

Page 68

Do it!

Answers could include:

1   I agree with the statement that says *abortion is wrong, but I think that abortion is sometimes the lesser of two evils in cases of rape or fatal foetal abnormality.*

2   Many people think it is acceptable *to get divorced in cases of adultery.*

3   I disagree with this because *I think that gay couples can make excellent parents.*

4   I can understand why some people agree with this; *however…*

5   I completely disagree with this because…

Page 69

Do it!

Answers will be personal responses.

Index